OVERCOMING

the

NEVERS

OVERCOMING
the
NEVERS

by Gardening Your Life *and*
Nurturing Seeds of Truth

TERI JOHNSON

Published by Advantage, Charleston, South Carolina.
Member of Advantage Media Group.

ADVANTAGE is a registered trademark and the Advantage colophon is a trademark of Advantage Media Group, Inc.

Printed in the United States of America.

ISBN: 978-1-59932-251-3
LCCN: 2011939728

This publication is designed to provide accurate and authoritative information in regard to the subject matter covered. It is sold with the understanding that the publisher is not engaged in rendering legal, accounting, or other professional services. If legal advice or other expert assistance is required, the services of a competent professional person should be sought.

Advantage Media Group is proud to be a part of the Tree Neutral® program. Tree Neutral offsets the number of trees consumed in the production and printing of this book by taking proactive steps such as planting trees in direct proportion to the number of trees used to print books. To learn more about Tree Neutral, please visit **www.treeneutral.com**. To learn more about Advantage's commitment to being a responsible steward of the environment, please visit **www.advantagefamily.com/green**

Dedicated to... YOU.

{each person who chooses to walk with me – may your heart be touched in a powerful way.}

Acknowledgements

Giving thanks with a grateful heart…

… to my mom and dad, Ron and Sandi Fitch; thank you for never giving up on me and for demonstrating unconditional love. Thank you for allowing me to experience life and for providing me with a solid foundation. Thank you for always encouraging me to do my best, and for raising me to believe that all things are possible. I love and appreciate you both very much.

… to Sara Buboltz, for encouraging me to pick up Susie Larson's book, *The Uncommon Woman*. My journey to overcome started there. Thank you.

… to Susie Larson, for planting seeds through your words into my heart, to be the uncommon woman God created me to be. You were the first one to plant the book writing seed in my mind when you replied to my email, "I'd love to use your story in my next book. You'd receive a writing credit for when you decide to write your own book. Hint hint. :)" I look forward to meeting you! Thank you.

… to my two special angels, Kathryn Cashman and Regan Sharpe. Thank you for walking in obedience and for speaking truth into my life at the perfect time. My life has been forever changed because of your willingness to love me through my ickiness.

… to my two first-class connections, Tom Endersbe and Denise Heintz. Nothing in God's world happens by mistake. You both have inspired me; thank you.

… to Glen Lerner; thank you for the introduction to Advantage and for the stimulating conversations. You've challenged me in unique ways – I appreciate you and our family friendship.

… to the girls who reviewed my first outline; Kristen Miller, Leah Mickschl, Jill Edlund, and Brandi Fitch. It was a mess, I know it! Thank you for the time you invested in me from the very beginning. Sister-friends is what you are. I love you!

… to my "cheerleading squad," who encouraged me when I was too weary to press on, and who lifted me up through my many tears on this journey; Susan Armfield, Shelbi Awabdy, Yolanda Harris, Barb Hadacek, Kim Leqve, Wendy Lynch, Deanna McGee, Denise Nelson, Tricia Riggin, Andrea Stephens, and Sarah Zolecki. Each word of support, each affirmation, each time you sincerely inquired about my progress, fueled me to persevere. Thank you.

… to my priceless gift when I needed you most, Patty Hemming-sen; thank you for your hard work and dedication to my family. Between all that you did and contributed to us during those short 6 months, you took the time to listen as I read random pieces out loud, and you were a great sounding board. Thank you for believing in me.

… to my brother Keith Robert Fitch, your perspective came at the most crucial time; "Remember it's God's timing, not ours." Thank you for reminding me of this when I was feeling overwhelmed and anxious about meeting deadlines. I love you.

…to my prayer warrior, Fay Herzog. What a wise spiritual mentor you are to me. Thank you for your ministry, your selflessness, your loving "all my personalities" and for pouring into me when my cup is empty. You are a blessing to me and so many.

… to Jessica Lynch, my patient niece. Thank you for pouring your heart and soul into the book trailer video. God has blessed you in so many ways. I love your passion and creativity. I am proud to be your auntie.

… to my virtual editor, Denise Weston; thank you for faithfully walking this journey with me, reviewing each chapter. Your kind words each step of the way were instrumental to me. I can't wait to meet you some day and give you a big hug. I truly appreciate you.

… to everyone who I've been blessed to work with on the Advantage team, thank you for your patience. What a gift to have such a talented, professional team of people behind me on this project. And to Brooke White, a special thank you for your grace, your understanding, and the encouragement you offered.

… to Rebekah Johnson my "keeping it personal" connection – you are a blessing to me. I truly appreciate the time you devoted to the questions after each chapter. I love how we are choosing to grow together, and challenging others to do the same. You are a bright light – thank you.

… to my precious nuggets, Zane and Zachary. Just thinking of you brings a smile to my face and joy into my heart. Thank you for all your questions, your love, your understanding, and your patience. I love you both so very much. I am so proud that God chose me to be your mom.

… to my greatest friend, my biggest fan, my amazing husband, Brent Johnson. Thank you for accepting me through it all, and for encouraging me to seek God's will and plan for my life. Thank you for believing in me when I didn't believe in myself and for comforting me through my refining moments. It's been a roller coaster ride, our journey together, but there is no one else I'd rather be strapped in with. I'm extremely grateful that God gave me you. I like you and I love you.

… to my heavenly Father, my Strength, my Healer, my One and only Source, my Provider – You put each and every one of these words on my heart. You were the writer of this book. Thank You for giving me "enough" daily. Thank You for graciously carrying me through each pain to experience joy and peace on the other side. You alone deserve all credit for this book. May every reader meet You in a sweet and special way as they turn each page. I love You.

Contents

*"I do not understand what I do. For what I want
to do I do not do, but what I hate I do."*
— ROMANS 7:15 NIV

Escape from Neverland.
What are the nevers?

THE NEVERS are the things we thought we'd never do or never experience. They could be a situation you never thought you'd be in, or a place you never imagined you'd be. We've all got them.

You've most likely heard the phrase, "Never say never." Have you said or thought that for yourself?

There are two types of Nevers. First are the good Nevers; the ones you'd like to put on your resume, the ones you've accomplished that make you feel proud and allow you to shine like a star. For example, you never thought that you'd graduate from a particular school with a 4.0 GPA, but you did! You never thought that you'd be hired for a particular position, but you were! Or, let's say you set out to run a marathon, never dreaming that you had what it takes to qualify for the Boston Marathon, but you did! These are good Nevers. With hard work, determination, and desire, we can accomplish the good Nevers, things that we thought were out of our reach, things we believed might be too good to be true, or that we were incapable of achieving. Accomplishing good Nevers brings us great satisfaction, joy, confidence, accolades, pride, excitement, and strength. We want to share these Nevers with others. They are empowering and can serve as platforms to achieve other great things. They are rewarding.

Then there are the other Nevers – the negative Nevers. These are ones you'd rather erase from your mind, press the delete button on, and run away from. You never thought that you'd get divorced, but you did. You never thought that you would get an abortion, but you did. You never thought you would become a victim of rape, but you were. You never dreamed that you would find yourself in an abusive relationship, but you're in one. You never thought that you would need to lose 200 lbs., but you do. You never thought that you'd be 45 years old and without a job, losing your home, and drowning in debt, but you are. These are negative Nevers. They come with feelings of regret, embarrassment, insecurity, guilt, and shame. They can become stumbling blocks and obstacles in our lives. They are troubling.

The Nevers that we will focus on in this book are the ones that stem from our list of disappointments and mishaps; the "bad things" that we'd hoped not to experience, not to do; the negatives.

Where do the Nevers come from?

The Nevers don't come out of nowhere. We're all born into a family of some kind or another. Some of us are raised by our biological birth parents. Some of us are adopted. Stepparents or grandparents raise some of us. Whoever we're raised by, whoever has the most impact in our lives – it could be older brothers and sisters, it could be pastors or teachers – in all cases we're instructed on what to do and what not to do. We learn, gain knowledge, and are influenced by these people in our world.

As we grow up and move through our life, we form opinions, judgments, and certain ideas about what life should look like. These come from our influencers, our environment and, for many of us, from religion. We decide what we want to accomplish. We imagine the things we would like to do. We dream about who we want to be. We explore what kinds of lives we want to live. We make decisions along the way based upon these ideas, and determine what we will and will not do. At some point, these lists of do's and don'ts, the will's and won'ts, our ideas of what's right and what's wrong, start to create our list of Nevers.

Then the dreadful day comes where we accomplish or experience our first negative Never. We do something that we vowed, spoke, or committed that we would never do. Sometimes we can move past these Nevers, seemingly unaffected, but as we get older, our file folder labeled, "The things I never thought I would experience," starts to get bigger.

With the bigger file folder comes a lot of lingering after-effects; negative feelings and negative thoughts, such as regret, embarrass-ment, fear, guilt, and insecurity, to name a few. These effects can cause us to start to believe lies about ourselves, such as: *I'm not good enough; I'm a bad person; I'm a loser; I must not be like other people because I keep doing things wrong; I am a failure.* The list of the destructive feelings we get from doing or experiencing the things we never thought we would, can be long.

Why is this a problem?

Our feelings effect our emotions, our emotions impact our thoughts, and our thoughts direct our attitude and our life direction. If our feelings about these experiences are destructive based on what we've come to believe, we are blinded and separated from the Truth about who God created us to be.

I can distinctly remember the first time I was dishonest and told a lie. Okay, this may not have been the very first time, but it's a time I clearly remember doing something that I never wanted to do.

I was in first grade. A classmate of mine dropped the string that belonged in the hood of her sweatshirt. I picked it up. I knew exactly whose it was and I knew the right thing to do; to give the string back to my classmate. But instead, I took the string, hid it in my cardboard school box, and proceeded to unravel it. As it was unraveled, it got "poufy." Towards the end of the day, my classmate was upset that she had lost her string, and the teacher asked the class if anyone had seen it. Everyone, including me, said "No." I lied! I had seen it, I had destroyed it and the evidence was in my cardboard pencil box.

I instantly knew that I had done something wrong, but I was fearful and didn't want anyone to know. Then the teacher asked everyone to open their backpacks and pencil boxes for her to check. POOF! There it came, popping out – and I was caught. I lied, I was dishonest, I was disrespectful to another person's property, and I was wrong.

The teacher disciplined me for that act and all the other students knew it. I had to sit inside for three days of recess. I can remember the kids looking through the window of my classroom while they were outside, at me inside. I felt shame. I felt embarrassment. I felt guilt. That was a Never accomplished; I'd never wanted to lie, but I had lied.

How did I deal with that? I can't remember. But I do know that I was not equipped. Every time I saw the classmate whom I had disrespected, or every time another schoolmate reminded me of the incident, I instantly felt terrible again. I wanted to hide. The lies I began to believe about myself were: *I am stupid; I am bad; I am not good enough.* The feelings I was left with were regret, shame, and embarrassment. Wow – that's a lot for one little 6-year-old girl!

I knew better, but we sometimes do the things that we don't want to do. This is just one small example of how our "Never" file folder starts to expand; it may seem trivial to you, but over time doing the Nevers, or getting to places you never planned on being, becomes more than just a laundry list of broken prohibitions because of the lingering effects they have on us.

How do the lingering effects of the Nevers manifest in our lives?

I wish there was one answer to this question – that would make it easy to overcome – but there is not; there are thousands!

A big brush-stroke picture includes effects like: insecurity, fear, people-pleasing, anger, depression, anxiety, feelings of not being good enough, believing you are undeserving, feeling that you're of less value than others, feeling insignificant, and needing constant approval from others. These are just some of the symptoms or manifestations of what the negative Nevers cause us.

Taking this one step further, for some people these feelings lead them to want to break away from the pain. Escaping leads to unhealthy coping mechanisms that can result in addictions such as eating disorders, excessive drinking of alcohol, or abusing drugs, both prescription and non-prescription, excessive shopping or spending, exercising too much, compulsive gambling, hording, compulsive lying, cutting, even working too much. This is a vicious cycle, because even if the addiction is removed, we still have the core issues, the painful feelings, and the raw emotions that we do not want to experience.

These issues are what lead us to live lives of discontentment and to suffer a restless desire or craving for something we do not have. Why? Because, we came to believe things about ourselves that were not true.

We must get to a point at which we can separate ourselves from the lingering after-effects. We need to decide to let go of the past hurts, regret, and pain that keep us stuck, that keep us circling the same issues. Shining the light on and uncovering the lies that are contained within our file folder of Nevers will bring healing to our wounds. We need to be set free; we need to experience freedom.

How do we experience freedom? I started to experience freedom while overcoming. It wasn't easy, I have to admit. But the joy and peace I have now far surpasses the work that it has taken me to get where I am today, and the work that I continue to do to sustain it.

Would you like to overcome and become who God created you to be? Do you have the desire to experience freedom? If so, walk with me. I am passionate about helping others and would be honored to share with you the tools that I've learned, and help you learn how to use them in your life to overcome the Nevers.

Discover truth. Embrace love. Experience joy.

Chapter 1

❖❖

WILLINGNESS

*"What we call the secret of happiness is no more a
secret than our willingness to choose life."*
— LEO F. BUSCAGLIA

Discovering truth. Embracing love. Experiencing joy.
Freedom starts with willingness. You have to want
this for yourself. There is no one who can decide for
you, or do the work on your behalf, or twist your arm.
Willingness is readiness. It doesn't have to come with loads of enthusiasm and extreme eagerness. It can start with a very small desire;
simply being willing to be willing.

I was desperate and I needed to find out how to experience
freedom. My life had become a mess and what I was doing was not
working for me. I mustered up small bits of willingness and, when I
was willing, God was able.

I had no idea what throwing my hands up in the air, surrendering my plans, my will, my ideas, my pride, and my motives meant
or looked like, but I was done and ready to get off the winding road.

Looking back, I can see now that God had been preparing me for that specific time of reaching bottom in my life. Several months prior, He had me stumble across a book through my friend's sister, called *The Uncommon Woman* by Susie Larson. Just the name of the book struck a chord in my heart – *The Uncommon Woman*. That is what I wanted to be. I picked up the book and devoured it. I read it not only once, but twice. I chewed on every chapter. I had the passion in my heart to possess the characteristics of the woman described in the book.

But, me? I can't be that woman, I'm not good enough! The tapes would play over and over in my mind of all the horrible things I'd done. I carried around shame from the Nevers I had experienced. I was not proud of the things I was currently doing, the impure thoughts that I had, or the prejudices and judgmental attitudes I stored in my mind. Simply put, I felt undeserving. *Look at me, who am I?* I had done a really great job in my life of accomplishing most of the Nevers that I'd vowed I would never do.

In April 2009, I got a call from a dear friend of mine, a mentor and a wise woman whom I admired. She wanted to have coffee with me. We had a chance to catch up and I shared with her the book I had read. It intrigued her and she asked if we could do a "book club" with the book together. I thought, *wow, my third time reading this book, really?* It took me only a brief second to respond, "Okay, I'm in – when do we start?" We decided that we would meet every Thursday morning and discuss a chapter each week. I was so excited!

The following week, we started. Before we dug in, my wise friend asked me a profound question. She said, "What can you give up and surrender in your life over the next few weeks, as we go through this book? Something that will free your mind and allow you to focus as you read; to really get the most out of what you're reading?" As I thought about her question, she shared with me what she was willing to "lay down." Then, I responded with my answer, "I will lay down alcohol – for the next 12 weeks, I will not drink alcohol."

I was excited about this commitment, because I knew that this was what I needed; accountability. In the back of my mind, I had been a little concerned about the amount of alcohol I had been drinking. I loved, loved, loved to unwind at night with a glass of wine. But the problem was that it wasn't just one night a week, it was more often seven, and it wasn't just one glass of wine, it was more often one bottle or two. So, that day, I did two things: I committed to not drink for an extended period of time, from the bottom of my heart – and I broke my commitment. That night, I drank so much wine that I passed out.

I wore the "shirt of shame" and the "pants of guilt" for the next three weeks when I met again with my wise friend. A day didn't go by that I didn't have a drink. She didn't ask about my commitment, and I didn't tell. I was dishonest and in fear. I was fearful of what she would think of me and afraid of what I had discovered. I was in bondage to alcohol and it was controlling my life.

On the morning of Tuesday, May 12th, 2009, I set out to accomplish one thing; pick out tile and granite for our home. The reality of what happened that day is this; I started drinking at noon and by 6:00 pm I was passed out, tucked safely into my bed. I didn't realize it at the time, but that was to be my last drink, by the grace of God.

I felt physically miserable when I woke up on Wednesday, May 13th. I vowed again that morning for the millionth time, "I will never drink again." I looked in the mirror and hated who I was becoming, and the place I was. I hated myself and my life. I couldn't take the extreme emotional pain I was experiencing any longer. I wanted to go to sleep and not wake up. I wanted to die. My life was out of control. I had come to a very low and lonely place; I had hit bottom.

The small bits of willingness I had mustered up gave me hope and strength to press on. I looked back to my Facebook status for that day and here's what I had posted:

May 13th, 2009 at 4:40pm via Facebook – Teri Fitch Johnson
is... I've got the joy, joy, joy, joy down in my heart...

WOW – only God could have given me the joy I felt on that day, the knowledge to know I had it "down in my heart" and the strength to do what I had to do the following day. I had to be honest with my accountability partner, my wise friend with whom I was doing the book club.

As we sat down to start discussing our book, I began by saying, "I will never find the freedom that is talked about in this book." I started to cry and through my tears I continued, "I have been dishonest with you. I haven't been able to not drink alcohol. I've been drinking since we started, and I don't know what to do."

We closed our books. We talked openly and honestly about my struggle. We discussed options. I made a decision. I made a phone call and admitted myself into an inpatient treatment facility for alcoholism. The decision was easy for me to make, but it came with a thousand mixed feelings. Yet, I was willing. God answered my prayers and all the details fell into place.

Today, I live life without alcohol – only because of Him. Yes, I am an alcoholic. I've embraced this as an asset, and have had the privilege of helping others who struggle with the same issue. However, this does not define me. Why? Because I'm made up of hundreds of other imperfections, good qualities, and experiences; alcoholism just happens to be one of them.

Through this experience, God has revealed to me my true passion, and for that I am forever grateful. It seems that each day different pieces of my "life puzzle" fall into place as I continue to be willing.

I was escaping from the lingering effects of accomplishing many negative Nevers by drinking alcohol. Alcohol had become my coping mechanism; it had become my addiction, my security blanket. Alcoholism had become one of my Nevers. I never thought I would be an alcoholic.

Being set free from alcohol was just the beginning for me. I needed to get to the root of all the issues that drove me to escape and cope in unhealthy ways; that was next. I had a lot of work to do, but I continued to maintain an attitude of willingness. I continued to choose life.

If we are open to doing things differently, if we are open to being honest with ourselves, if we are willing to do what it takes to discover truth, the blinders will be lifted. We will recognize what we need to do, and we can experience freedom.

Discovering God's plan for you is possible. Freedom, a good future, and hope are available for you. Are you willing to be willing?

> *"Trust in the LORD with all your heart and lean not on your own understanding; in all your ways submit to Him, and He will make your paths straight."*
>
> —**Proverbs** 3:5-6 NIV

I am willing – now what?

You will need to do something different than what you've been doing. Implement the dreaded six-letter word; change.

> *"Insanity: doing the same thing over and over again and expecting different results."* —ALBERT EINSTEIN

If you can relate to this concept of insanity, continuously circling the same mountain expecting to get different results; if the lingering after-effects of the Nevers are contaminating your thoughts, relationships, and career; then you need to embrace a new method. You need to consider living life differently, and to find new tools to help you. That's what I needed, new tools.

When I arrived at the alcohol treatment facility and finished the extensive admissions process, I was lonely and scared. My mind raced with thoughts of my kids, the man that I loved, and my life. How could I be gone from my world for 28 days? Was I being selfish to take this time for me? I had no idea what this experience would be like, but I was willing. I was open-minded and ready to stop the insanity, whatever that meant.

I was introduced to a special tool box when I was in treatment, tools that had been helping people since 1939 – the 12 Steps of Alcoholics Anonymous. As I dug into the "Big Book" where the 12 Steps were contained and started reading them, I thought to myself, *okay, step one got it, check – step two, I'm getting this, got it, check, step three, yep, got that too! Wow, this is great – I'm such a quick study, I've got this thing going on; bring it! I'm breezing right on through these steps and it's only my second day. Yippee!*

After 28 days of working on me, and working through many of my negative Nevers, I was so excited to go home and see my family.

But honestly I was scared to live my life without drinking alcohol. I had heard story after story while in treatment from others who had relapsed; I was nervous. The stories scared me enough that I knew I didn't want that to happen to me.

I decided that I was going to do whatever it took not to drink. Period. Whatever I thought it took. What I thought it would take was not drinking! Right? That was the problem, right? Alcohol?

It didn't take me much time to discover I was wrong. I figured it out when I met a woman by the name of Towanda. Who was Towanda? Towanda was Teri. She was me without alcohol – and she was nasty!

Before I continue, I have to say this. If your name is Towanda and you're reading this, please do not take offense. I grabbed the name from a scene that I remembered from the movie *Fried Green Tomatoes*. Actress Kathy Bates plays the character Evelyn Couch and gives her alter ego this name.

I hadn't followed any of the recommendations given to me from the treatment facility for my aftercare plan; I was simply not drinking. I wasn't tapping into any of the tools that were introduced to me, and my "Big Book" from Alcoholics Anonymous hadn't been opened since the day that I'd driven off the campus of the treatment facility. I was doing life alone. I was discontent, irritable all the time, and restless. I thought drinking was my problem – so why, when I'd stopped drinking, was I still so miserable?

Little did I know that I was dealing with a force to be reckoned with called pride; p-r-i-d-e, and oh, was it poisonous! What I didn't grasp was that I was miserable because I was full of pride and because of my pride and my ego, which I'd named Towanda, I was unable to tap into the tool box.

I thought that I was doing such a great job of not drinking. I thought that I could do it; I thought that I was strong. I knew what was right for me and I thought I knew what would make everyone in my life happy, so I continued to keep doing what I was doing. I directed it all; I was in control. If everyone would do what I thought they should do, then I would be happy, right?

That is where I was wrong. We lived with Towanda for 8 months. Many people refer to this phase that I'm talking about as the "dry drunk"; unfortunately, that was me. I was still miserable, and I didn't know why. I was white-knuckling my way through life without my solution, my coping mechanism, which was alcohol and, again, I wanted to die.

Now I have a greater appreciation for – and understanding of – why people relapse. I am not surprised that people do, if they're feeling as miserable as I had been feeling.

Then, on February 13, 2010, God brought me another angel who spoke truth into my life. I had only met this person one time prior to this mini-intervention with Towanda, and I didn't know her very well, but she too was in recovery.

As we started to talk about my recovery, I told her that I was just not drinking. Great recovery work, huh? She saw Towanda in me and said, "Girl, you need to take your claws out of life! You are miserable, you are angry, it is written all over you and you do not wear it well. It is gross."

My initial thought to this bold, honest statement was, "Wow. Okay, blunt girl, you can just go home now!" As I processed what she said and let her words sink in, I knew that what she had spoken was what I needed to hear.

My question was *how?* I wanted to let go. I wanted to be free. I didn't want to be miserable, angry, and gross. I needed someone to show me how; I needed help.

By the end of the day, she asked me if she could help me implement the 12 Step toolbox into my life. I am grateful to her for reaching out to me. My ego and pride were blocking me from asking for help, but God prompted her to offer to help me and she was obedient. I humbly accepted, and the next day we started working the 12 Steps. She thoroughly guided me through each step and 4 days later, we were there, Step 12. What I called the "4-Day Boot Camp" changed my life! I was transformed from the inside. For the first time in my life, I sincerely surrendered my will and my plans to a Higher Power.

When I was willing, God was able. A miracle happened in my life during those 4 days; I will never be the same. I faced fears. I uncovered insecurities. I worked through resentments. God removed blockage from my life, and I found freedom.

I am so grateful for the very blunt way that God woke me up to this. I didn't have a pair of glasses on that allowed me to see the problem. Those who were close to me in my world walked on eggshells, and I could not understand why – until someone told me and I was willing to see it.

Since that boot camp experience, I've realized the importance of the 12 Step toolbox. The steps are not something that you "do"; they are a road map for living. They are valuable tools for ALL areas of life, and for all walks of life. Research has showed me that the 12 Steps have been adapted widely around the world by various groups of people dealing with addictions, hurts, compulsive behaviors, and mental health issues. Additionally, some groups have adapted parts of the 12 Step approach.

We are faced each day with challenges in relationships, with our children, and with our careers. We have loved ones getting ill or dying. We have to deal with others not living life the way that we would have them live it. We come across new resentments, things that make us angry. We've got loved ones, or even some of us personally, who are filing for bankruptcy, losing jobs, seeing our homes go into foreclosure, or are unable to pay rent. Every day we are presented with life, and we all have Nevers. These tools can help.

This is not just a toolbox; it's a valuable, life-changing toolbox that, once you experience it, you will not want to live without. Implementing the 12 Steps in your life might be the "something different" that you need to get different results. The 12 Steps are the basis of this book, and its inspiration. As you read through the following pages, I encourage you to look at these tools in this way. Instead of thinking of the Steps as something that you "do" allow them to guide the way in which you "live." Incorporate them into your world; check in daily to see where you are. You will begin to understand the meaning behind each tool by working them and personalizing them. You will start to know what tool you're missing or not working when you catch yourself reverting back to old feelings or behaviors.

Let me give you an example. A few months ago, I started to feel discontent. I noticed that my claws were slowly starting to come out again and dig into life. I was feeling anxiety over a decision that I knew needed to be made. I was worrying about the future, trying to predict the outcome of a few situations, and my stomach was in knots.

Each morning I have a routine of what I do with my quiet time—the books I read, my prayers, etc. But I was feeling as though I was just "going through the motions." I was feeling empty, not getting anything out of them. I felt as though my prayers were hitting the ceiling.

I decided to look into my toolbox, and go through each step, evaluating where I was. I felt pretty comfortable until I got to Step 11, "Sought through prayer and meditation to improve our conscious contact with God, as we understood Him, praying only for knowledge of His will for us and the power to carry that out." Awareness: this was it! This is where I'd been slacking. Pray and meditate, listen; that is what I was missing.

I wasn't listening to God. I wasn't taking the time to wait on Him. I was just checking the box; I was going through the motions, doing the minimum that needed to be done. I read my Bible and my devotional readings, quickly prayed, and then packed it all up to start my day. I wasn't listening.

My will, my agenda, and my direction started to slowly make their ways back into my life. Once I realized what I was missing, I was able to focus on that area and things got better.

This is important. When you start to feel uneasy inside, when the feelings of restlessness, discontentment, irritability, and control begin to rise up within you – how do you cope? What do you do? I've found a solution that works for me. I tap into my trusty toolbox; the 12 Steps.

Unfortunately, it took me about 9 months to realize these tools could help me once I had removed alcohol as my coping mechanism. Fortunately, I maintained the attitude of willingness and was able to hear truth from a friend.

Prior to entering the treatment facility, I was not familiar with the 12 Step program. When I researched how and by whom this program was being used I realized it was impacting many lives, not only those of alcoholics. This made sense to me once I was willing to incorporate the tools into my daily life.

This book isn't about alcoholism; that just happens to be my story. This book isn't only for the alcoholic; it is for anyone who has come to a point at which he or she is in some sort of pain. Whether it's a tremendous amount of pain which leads to addiction, or it's emotional pain and you're depressed, stuck, and don't know how to move forward, this book can help you.

Severe mental disorders like clinical depression or bipolar disorder are conditions that may go beyond implementation of these tools, and require professional intervention and possibly medication. If you feel you are experiencing these disorders, contact a physician or counselor for professional help.

If you're suffering from that kind of condition, and are stabilized, you're likely to have a lot of the lingering effects of hitting those Nevers that need to be dealt with. This book is for you, too – for anyone who could benefit from a surrender of the notion of "self," to what God's plan is for us.

There is a solution for overcoming the storm, the storm that the Nevers create. My Nevers are going to be totally different than yours, and yours are different than the person next to you. Mine might even seem trivial to you. But our Nevers are all the same, in that they all affect us equally, regardless if it's a big thing or, in someone else's eye, a little thing. The lingering effects influence us the same way. Let me share another personal example with you.

When I was in high school, and I had sex out of wedlock— I accomplished a Never. Had I gotten pregnant, would it have been a worse sin, or made me feel guiltier? No. I'd have had to deal with the public judgment of others, but the shame I felt coming from within me would have been the same. That's where our Nevers are. We don't need to feel the scorn of others to know that we've done wrong.

I'm not here to tell you you're a bad person for breaking your Nevers, even if they're totally different from mine. What I'm here to do is to help you break free of the lingering shame and guilt and bad feelings they've caused you, the feelings that sap your self-worth and keep you from being your best self.

It doesn't matter to me what you did. No Never accomplished or experienced is too big or too small. It just is what it is. You could have committed a murder; most of us are guilty of doing it in our heads. Can you relate? Have you ever sat across from somebody and thought, "Oh, my goodness, I could kill him right now"? In my dark, bitter days, I had that thought. Fortunately, most of us don't take action on our thoughts, but some do. Does that make that person worse than I am, for actually committing it when I just thought about it? I don't believe that it does. Of course, that person will suffer consequences for his or her behavior, just like I suffer consequences for my behavior. But it doesn't make him or her any less of a person than I, or undeserving of mercy and grace. It doesn't mean that that person can't receive the same joy, peace and forgiveness that is free for the asking, if you are willing to seek it out in your life.

Maintain an attitude of willingness and take action. Our life is a garden; whatever we feed and focus on grows. Chances are that there are many weeds that need to be removed. When we start to get down to the roots of what those weeds are, it might not be pretty. It means getting in touch with our feelings, understanding why we do the things that we do, and sometimes that's a place we don't want to go. It won't be easy digging up the root instead of just chopping down the weed. But until you dig deep and get the root out, the weed just keeps coming back.

As we go through this journey together and start overcoming our Nevers, you may want to quit. Don't give up; press on! As we plant new seeds, we will learn to care for them, and not let the bad weeds claim our attention.

Are you willing? Simply willing to be willing? If so, walk with me. Turn the page, continue on. Let's journey together willingly.

Keeping it Personal

1. Are you "willing to be willing?" If so, GREAT! If not, what is holding you captive? What is it that keeps you hanging on?

2. Sometimes it's difficult to admit to our Nevers. Sometimes we have to take baby steps. Identify one Never that you have experienced. Just one. Identifying is a BIG help in letting go.

3. Teri talks about "small bits" of willingness giving her joy. If you have the willingness, have you identified the JOY you are experiencing, even in some small way?

4. I don't know what Never you are experiencing or have experienced, but write out your thoughts after reading Teri's testimony. Do you feel encouraged? Are you thinking that perhaps you can do it, that perhaps you, too, can OVERCOME with God's help? Write it down!

5. What "weeds" are in your life? Have you plucked off the stems, or have you dug out the root? What have you "planted" in your life to take the place of those weeds?

Chapter 2

ACCEPTANCE

Step 1:
We admitted we were powerless over {life, others, emotions}
alcohol — that our lives had become unmanageable.

My Tool:
I accept into my heart that I, ME, MYself – am NOT in control, and
that when I operate on my own, my life becomes unmanageable.
I become discontent, irritable, angry, frustrated.

*"Some people confuse acceptance with apathy, but there's
all the difference in the world. Apathy fails to distinguish
between what can and what cannot be helped; acceptance
makes that distinction. Apathy paralyzes the will-to-action;
acceptance frees it by relieving it of impossible burdens."*
—ARTHUR GORDON

O kay. I am here. I've experienced a whole bunch of Nevers. I might be at a place where I never thought I'd be. I've identified that I don't feel really happy, or joyous, or free. I've identified that there are things seriously wrong in my life, and I'm probably hanging onto some shame, guilt, resentment, anger – something. I'm willing to learn new tools that will help set me free.

The first tool which we need to pick up is acceptance. This is the foundation upon which we will build and the tool that we need to tap into most frequently.

The myth about acceptance is that it shows weakness, because ultimately by truly accepting, we are admitting defeat. The reality is that accepting is acknowledging and understanding the scope of where we are. By acknowledging our powerlessness, we are actually empowered, and this cultivates strength.

When we take the knowledge that comes with accepting – which is to believe our reality, seeing the truth about our lives and allowing that truth to make the 12-inch drop from our heads into our hearts – then we can take action.

> *"Knowledge is Power."*
>
> —SIR FRANCIS BACON

What brings us to the point of acceptance? Everyone has different tolerance levels. What may seem overwhelming and unmanageable for me may seem like a piece of cake for you. Rest assured, we all have a breaking point. At that point, we realize that what we are doing is not working. We've tried "our way" numerous times, each attempt leaving us defeated. We've come to the conclusion we can't do this on our own anymore; we are out of answers.

Ask yourself the following questions...

* Do you feel like you're carrying the weight of the world on your shoulders?

* Are you feeling out of control in relationships, at work, or with your family members?

* Have you lost focus on the things which you believe to be important, because you're doing things that others feel are important?

* Are you compromising yourself to satisfy or please others?

* Are you embarrassed, or feeling guilt and/or shame about past mistakes?

* Are you carrying around the baggage from things that happened years ago? Days ago?

* Do you feel like you don't know who you are? Do you wonder, *what is my purpose?*

* Do you have a difficult time saying "no" to others, when asked to do something?

* Are you constantly seeking the approval of others?

Did you answer YES to any or all of these questions? If so, you might be getting close to your breaking point, or potentially you have already arrived.

In his book, *A Hunger for Healing*, J. Keith Miller shares other ways in which we may reach the point of acceptance. "In the end it is usually the pain of our compulsions, addictions, and denial and the resulting strained or broken relationships that drive us to the stark awareness of our powerlessness. Unfortunately it may take a tragedy or crisis to break through our delusion of power – a divorce, a family member's addiction, a runaway child, a terminal illness, a bankruptcy, a death."

In addition to the subjects of these questions, painful experiences, and unfortunate situations, extreme feelings such as anger, frustration, discontentment, sadness, loneliness, anxiety, and jealousy can bring us to a place of hopelessness.

If you get to this end place, if you are currently living in this end place, if the life you're living is full of unacceptable things to you, then your only answer is acceptance. The alternative is to keep doing what you're doing – which means that you will keep getting what you're getting, and you will keep feeling what you're feeling.

When I accept, I'm not saying, "Everything is okay, life is perfect." I am not saying that I condone behavior that is inappropriate. I am not saying that something is right when it clearly is wrong. I am not saying that I deserve to be punished unfairly, or to be abused. What I am saying is that, whatever my issues are – an unhappy marriage, an unexpected loss, a lousy job, disrespectful kids, unloving friends, an abusive relationship – whatever my situation is – I need to look in the mirror.

Acceptance starts with me! Something that is happening right now is not working, or does not feel good. I am upset, and experiencing things I never thought I would experience – in short, I cannot control my life. I cannot change others. I can only start by taking responsibility for myself, and for my attitude. For a lot of people, the concept of accepting responsibility is daunting and scary. It means that you have to finally stop putting blame on other people for your situation, and accept it for what it is.

This may sound harsh. You may have been programmed to believe differently, but you must accept life on life's terms. Life is not fair. Life is hard. You may not like the cards that you were dealt, but accepting life on life's terms is crucial to our emotional well-being and forward progress. When we discover a person, place, thing, or situation that is unacceptable to us, we need to take out our acceptance tool. That is the crucial point at which we need to make a choice. Am I choosing to live positively? Or am I choosing to live negatively? The situation may not be exactly what I thought it would be, but I have to accept and acknowledge that this is the way it is. And then I have to decide, *what am I going to do?* How will I respond, and with what attitude will I decide to move forward?

Expecting others to change just because I want them to change is unrealistic and wishful thinking. We can't make others change; we can only change ourselves. Do you have the strength to make the changes necessary to turn a situation around through an attitude of acceptance? Or will you remain powerless, remain in the state of non-acceptance and let everything around you dictate how you feel? I can't change somebody else. Period.

What can you look forward to, once you embrace the positive attitude of acceptance in your life?

Rising above. Growth. Change in others. Strength. Once you accept it in your heart, not just your

> *"Consider how hard it is to change yourself and you'll understand what little chance you have in trying to change others."*
>
> – UNKNOWN

head, this attitude gives you the power and the strength to pull up your bootstraps and get to work—to take action, to garden your life. This is where it can get tough. Planting new seeds and digging up the roots of what got you to the places you never thought you'd be is essential intentional work that needs to be done, because if you don't take a different course of action, your future is going to look just like your past. It's going to play out over and over, in just the same, tired way.

Some think taking action is changing the external circumstances. Take the person who hates his job. His boss doesn't treat him right, his coworkers are slackers – so he quits and gets another job. And – surprise! – it's the same thing all over again; another bad boss, another group of useless coworkers. Many people repeat this pattern several times. They hop from job to job, hoping the next situation will be better than the last, and it's not. We've all seen the type; we might even *be* the type. What does that tell you?

Wherever you go, there you are. The problem isn't following you – you are the problem. I shared previously that I thought my problem was drinking. Let's use this as another example. I could have said, "Okay, I'm just going to move, because in this environment, I am drinking way too much alcohol. I'm surrounded by a crowd of friends who enjoy drinking. I'm surrounded by the experiences that trigger me to want to drink. To solve my drinking problem, I will just move, and then I will be fine." Say I pick up and move to a different state. But, whoops – there's alcohol there, too. And maybe I start to think, "Oh, I'm in a different state. I could probably drink here, and be okay. It's a new place, new people. I'll be different too." But guess what? Alcohol is my coping mechanism. So, no matter what, I'm going to escape from my issues with drinking, because that's what I'm using to make myself feel better. And – *boom* – I'm back where I started. Because the problem wasn't where I was, it's who I am. It's me. I am an alcoholic. In this scenario, I am not accepting my alcoholism; instead I am manipulating my surroundings in an effort to get different results. This is denial.

Similar things happen with people who are negative and who are complainers. No matter what they do – dump their friends for new ones, change their lives on a superficial basis – the real problem is their own negativity, a reflection of how they feel about themselves, about what's going on inside their heart. Most often, these people see themselves as "forever" victims. Until they accept that fact, they're not going to be able to change. Why? Because everywhere I am, I am. And I am the problem.

We are our biggest problem. Of all the fears that are out there in the world, accepting that you're the problem might just be the hardest one to face. It is a scary place for some of us, because it's all we've known. If we can no longer blame our unhappiness on some outside force, what do we have?

Remove the problem. Remove the escape. Remove the excuses. Remove blaming others. What is left? It's just me, and now I have to look at myself and say, *Whoa. Who am I really? I am wrong. What character traits do I need improvement on? What is the truth – what will it take for me to discover my truth?*

As you can see, attempting to change the external with the acceptance tool is merely a Band-Aid and won't do the job. The action we must take is internal; this is where we will start to reap life-changing benefits that are sustainable.

What does the internal action of acceptance look like? Let me share a story to help you understand. A friend of mine is in a season of change. Things are happening in her life that are unplanned and out of her control. Her husband had an opportunity to become partner in his law firm. This was very exciting for them; their dreams were becoming reality, and doors of opportunity were opening. The financial investment alone for this step forward was a major under-taking, not to mention the greater commitment to the organization and new partners.

Expecting that the hard work and financial investment would reap great rewards, they were extremely disappointed when they were notified that instead of receiving a quarterly dividend to cushion their bank account or to pay for the new furniture for which they had been patiently waiting, they had to scrounge up a large amount of money to pay into the business. Unfortunately, in the last quarter, their firm had lost money. This just didn't seem right, my friend shared with me. For years, the firm had rewarded the partners each quarter. Now, the first quarter her husband made partner, *this* happens? She explained that her husband had chosen to work harder in order to show his commitment to the firm, at the expense of the family – and for what? Where would they find the funds to pay in? She was angry. This was unacceptable. It was not fair!

Let's pause here for a moment. These are the feelings (frustra-tion, disappointment, irritation) that we need to recognize. This is our prompting moment to pick up our acceptance tool. There is pain, confusion, and anger. We have a choice to make. Negative: Will we harbor this, sulk in this, let these feelings take root, feed them and allow them to grow and contaminate our life? Or positive: Look in the mirror, peel back the layers and identify why we are so upset, reflect on the situation, and move forward with acceptance, taking internal action.

This is what positive internal action looks like; let's take another look at the story. While talking this situation through with my friend we were able to discover some positives. Although these were difficult financial times, we were able to peel back the layers and get to the root of their motives, their whys, and their expectations.

Here's what we found. They were putting important things on the back burner, such as time with the kids, and their time and relationship with each other, in order to gain approval at the firm and to earn and reap the benefits that come from being a partner; essentially, trying to look good. What they expected from this hard work and sacrifice was a monetary payoff.

The problem with this type of motivation (approval, people pleasing) is that we will most likely always be disappointed. The solution? Accepting their situation, acknowledging there is nothing they can do to change it. It is what it is. Life is on life's terms. Internally, they can learn from it by using it as a stepping-stone for growth, and take action to realign what's fundamentally important. Eliminating their expectations and accepting the reality that every future quarter at the firm could be different financially, will not pull the rug out from under their feet. The lesson learned here is to work according to your comfortable level of commitment, to the degree that allows you to balance your priorities. Then, regardless of the outcome, you won't feel cheated. Your heart is in the right place.

Here are a few more scenarios to show you how to implement the acceptance tool:

You didn't get accepted to the medical school to which you'd applied this year.

Feelings: *Rejection, fear, not good enough, insecure, embarrassed.*

Negative: *I will never get in, just my luck, this will never happen. OR – I'm not good enough, of course they didn't accept me – others are more qualified and better than me.*

Positive: *What can I do to increase my chances of getting accepted next year? Now I have an opportunity to work and save money, grow, and learn new things that will give me experience.*

Your spouse lost his/her job and he/she is doing nothing about getting a new one.

Feelings: *Disrespected, as though you're being taken advantage of, anger, resentment, fear, as though you're unimportant.*

Negative: *Constantly nag your spouse about getting off his/her lazy butt to get a job. Make comments and snide remarks about your spouse to others. Complain about your financial situation, have a pity-party, live resentfully.*

Positive: *Lovingly communicate your concern, the reality of the situation and your true feelings to your spouse. Set specific boundaries that are acceptable to you and determine what will happen if the boundaries are not kept. Follow through.*

A relationship with a friend has become distant because she had a baby.

Feelings: *Resentment, abandonment, loneliness, rejection, sadness.*

Negative: *Why did she get to have a baby and I can't get pregnant? Our lives are going in different directions; it's not the same when we are together anymore, it's all about the baby.*

Positive: *Find different new ways to stay connected that are respectful to her new role as a mother, and focus on the things that you still have in common.*

....

Through acceptance we can learn, we are humbled, and we are empowered. We can choose the action we will take in every situation. We can identify our roles and other's roles, and grow. Acceptance is the start of freedom. This simple tool, if embraced, can open our eyes to see the truth, which allows us to make wise and sound decisions as we move forward.

A quick snapshot on the acceptance tool is this; I acknowledge that acceptance starts with me and me alone. Taking action isn't changing everything around us, although that might need to happen. We may need to change in order to get out of an unhealthy or a compromising situation. But the necessary action we must take is looking within every time we feel pain, discontent, or fear. Let these negative feelings prompt us to dig deep and discover what we need in order to move through in a healthy way.

Remember, this is our first tool; it is our anchor, and one that we will continue to go back to. We've got several more that will help us move forward once we commit to wearing our accepting glasses when we start to feel that something in our life is unacceptable.

Keeping it Personal

1. Do you have the power that acceptance brings? What in reality are you refusing to accept?

2. Who/what are you blaming for your life? Is it YOU?

3. Name one person whom you want to change. Choose to let that person go. Choose to accept that person just the way that he or she is. Now, move on to the next one...

4. What unpleasant circumstance is in your day today? How can you change your thoughts to shine a ray of positivity on the situation?

5. Where is your heart? Where are your expectations? In the story of the husband who became a partner at the law firm, what differences in their hearts or their expectations could have made their journey less rocky? Can you relate that story to a personal story of your own?

C H A P T E R   3

FAITH

STEP 2:
Came to believe that a Power greater than ourselves could restore us to sanity.

MY TOOL:
I have confidence or faith that only God can calm my storm.
Only if I believe can I take action and act purposefully.

*"When you walk to the edge of all the light you have and take
that first step into the darkness of the unknown, you must believe
that one of two things will happen: There will be something solid
for you to stand upon, or, you will be taught how to fly."*

— PATRICK OVERTON

I continue to be willing to take action. I acknowledge that I am powerless, which in and of itself is empowering. But how do I sustain acceptance and the strength to restore myself from my fallen place? The answer is, I don't. This is where we pick up our next tool, faith.

To get a clearer understanding of what faith truly is, I think we need to start with the basics. The word gets thrown around so loosely at times. Do we really understand how much faith we have? Let's unpack the word so we can apply it to our lives.

Faith is confidence or trust in a person or thing, belief that is not based on proof. To have faith, it is not necessary to have proof. Proof is not the foundation. Faith comes from conviction, certainty, and hope.

Faith is trust, and trust is belief in something as true. It is reliance on the integrity, strength, ability, and surety of a person or thing; faith is confidence.

Faith is belief, and belief is assurance in the truth or existence of something not immediately susceptible to rigorous proof; faith is reliability.

These words – faith, trust, belief – are interchangeable. We all possess some form of faith. Let me give you one example of what this could look like. You see a seemingly comfortable but unfamiliar chair across a room, it looks reliable and sturdy, and you believe that the chair will hold you up. You trust that when you sit down, it will sustain your weight. You have faith that when you plant yourself in the unfamiliar chair, it will meet your need for comfort. So you proceed to sit down and yes, it does – it holds you up, it sustains your weight, it meets your needs. That is faith. Belief. Trust.

We put our faith, our trust, and our belief into hundreds of things daily. We trust people. We have faith in our employers. We have a belief that others will not run stop signs. We trust that the light will turn on when we flip the switch. We have faith that our spouse is committed to us. We believe that our children are telling us the truth. All things made by, inspired by, and created by God, we have faith in. But what about the Creator, the Source, God Himself? Do you put your faith, trust, and belief in Him?

Higher Power. God. I am not assuming that you believe in a Higher Power and I am not going to make the assumption that if you do, you have named your Higher Power, God. What I will assume is that, based on the definitions and example I've shared, you are capable of believing, trusting, and having faith, and that you've come this far into reading this book because you are looking for an answer, a solution or tools to help you calm a storm, give you peace, or to receive restoration and healing in your life.

Based on what I am assuming, I have a request. Would you consider shelving your opinions and judgments as you read the next few pages? Would you consider opening your mind as I share my faith journey with you? I am not a seminary graduate. I am not a pastor or an ordained minister. I have not been baptized or confirmed. I am simply a woman who has been wounded, who has carried around the lingering after-effects of the Nevers for many years, and now, a women who has experienced healing and an indescribable joy by coming to believe that a Power greater than me can restore me to sanity.

God was a very large part of the family into which I was born. I grew up going to church every Sunday morning, as well as most Sunday nights, and for the majority of my life, Wednesday nights too. From what I know, Christianity goes back in my family for generations. As a little girl, I accepted Jesus Christ into my heart and had always considered myself a Christian. I felt I knew who God was.

I can remember most of the Bible stories that I was taught in Sunday school, growing up. I can remember being told to read my Bible and pray every day, but that was a roller coaster ride for me. Sometimes I was really into it, and other times I was not. Most often, I was not. I didn't understand the Bible when I would attempt to read it, and when I would pray, I didn't feel a connection to God.

For me, God existed only at church. He was not personal to me. Through my viewpoint as a child, personal relationships were defined as those that I had with people whom I could see and touch, like my parents. I could talk with them and they would talk back to me; I didn't grasp or experience this personal-ness with God. What I received growing up, what was filtered into my head was this: God, church, the Bible, and religion all boiled down to a list of the do's and the don'ts.

I believed in God, yes. I had faith that what I was taught to do and the rules I was taught to obey were good for me and in my best interests. I trusted that if I did not obey the rules and the laws in the Bible, the 10 Commandments, I would go to Hell.

I tried so hard to do things right. I worked so hard to not screw up. The more I tried, the more I failed. The harder I worked, the more I felt that I was not good enough. Faith was religion. Faith was being at every church service. Faith was praying often and reading the Bible regularly. Faith was not working for me.

Again, I believed in God. But what had I come to believe about God? I believed that I was not worthy of God's love. I believed that only if I was obedient and not sinning, would He accept me and help me.

Here's the problem, I couldn't stop doing "wrong" things: I couldn't stop sinning. I couldn't stop experiencing Nevers. I couldn't break free from the cycle of insanity. Every time I attempted to change myself and experience God, I was tripped up by my humanness, my shortcomings, and my past.

This struggle started at a very young age. I can distinctly remember going to Bible camp in the summers. In between chasing boys and socializing, I would experience God. I would learn about His goodness, His love for me, and His forgiveness. Every summer, I would repent of my sins and make a promise to God that I would make the right choices from that point forward. I vowed to be good and obey the rules. I would leave camp with a renewed spirit, a renewed heart, and a plan to be the perfect Christian. But the minute I got home, I was back to my life, back to my same friends, and back to doing the same things that I did before I went to camp. My perfect plan didn't pan out to be so perfect; I failed. I was not worthy.

My spiritual growth stopped. I don't feel that I was ever equipped with the knowledge of how to take my God experience one step further. I didn't know how to sustain it, or how to incorporate God into my daily life. My feelings of guilt, shame, embarrassment, failure, and unworthiness blocked me from connecting with God, and by extension blocked me from discovering who God created me to be.

My God, my Higher Power, in whom I believed in for most of my life, was somebody that I feared. I didn't consistently do what

I thought He wanted me to do, and I couldn't figure out how to do what I wanted to do, to be good. So, I gave up trying. Eventually I stopped going to church, which made me feel guilty, because Christians are supposed to go to church. I stopped trying to pray, which I felt bad about too, because all good Christians pray. I stopped seeking acceptance from God and started seeking acceptance from others, my work, my relationships, and the world.

What did seeking acceptance this way look like for me? It was compromising my values, saying "yes" when my heart told me I should be saying "no." Stealing. Gossiping. Pre-marital sex, one-night stands. Dishonesty. Dabbling in marijuana and smoking cigarettes. Binge drinking. Going places I didn't want to go, and doing things I didn't want to do. People pleasing. Divorce. It was dark, it was lonely, it was out of control. It caused me to experience many hardships and heartaches, and many Nevers. It wounded my soul and defeated me. I think I looked okay from the outside, but inside of me, there was a raging war. Others influenced me, but not God.

Accepting Jesus in my heart, obeying the rules, adhering to the law, not breaking the 10 Commandments, and closely following a list of "do's" and "don'ts" is what having faith, believing in a Power greater than me, meant to me for over 30 years.

Then, one day not too long ago, I was driving alone in my truck heading home from who knows where, listening to the radio. I can recall the day like it was yesterday, especially the feelings of misery I had. I had a storm raging inside of me that could not be calmed. My life to my acquaintances and to those who did not live with me may have looked rosy – but behind closed doors in my personal dwelling place, both physically and mentally, my life had become unmanageable. I could not live like this any longer.

Live like this? What was "this"? What did that mean? I had been racking my brain trying to figure out what living like "this" meant. I was exploring what changes I could make in my world that would make me feel better. What could I do? At the time, I could not see. I was blind to everything. I had no answers. I thought that maybe if I traveled less, that would make me happy. Or, maybe if I exercised more, I would feel better. Or, if I was more organized or worked more or worked less or ate healthier… I had tried everything that I could think of, and nothing, no one thing, was bringing me joy. What I was doing was not working.

On that noteworthy day, as I was driving, I heard a song that I had heard no less than 100 times before. For some reason, the words spoke loudly to me that day. I cranked it up and started singing the words at the top of my lungs as tears streamed down my face.

I prayed these words to God as I sang them from the bottom of my heart, the cry of my heart. "My life has led me down the road that's so uncertain, and now I am left alone and I am broken, trying to find my way, trying to find the faith that's gone. This time, I know that you are holding all the answers. I'm tired of losing hope and taking chances, on roads that never seem to be the ones that bring me home. Give me a revelation, show me what to do, 'cause I've been trying to find my way, I haven't got a clue. Tell me should I stay here, or do I need to move – give me a revelation. I've got nothing without You." {*Revelation* by Third Day}

I was searching for purpose, clarity, and freedom. That prayer was the starting point of a new beginning on my faith journey. I sincerely drew near to God in those couple of minutes, and He started to draw near to me. I was so far away and disconnected from Him at that point, yet I had hope. During that encounter and by the grace of God I sensed that He, my Higher Power, could restore me. I didn't have proof yet. I hadn't experienced a change, and my problems were still just as real as they were before I cried out to Him. But in that moment, I came to believe. I came to trust, even though I didn't know what trust looked like. For the first time in many years, I had faith and confidence in a Power greater than me.

What was next? How could I take that moment and nurture it? I was reminded of the simplicity of two verses I had once heard: "Draw near to me, and I will draw near to you" (inspired by James 4:8a), and "Seek first the Kingdom of God and His righteousness and all these things will be added unto you" (inspired by Matthew 6:33). I decided that I could do that. I could draw near to Him. I could seek Him first. So I began, without proof, without evidence; I took baby steps and God worked with my mustard seed of faith.

I whispered "popcorn prayers" (random, short little prayer-whispers; talks with God throughout the day) when I was upset or confused. I said "thank you" prayers when I recognized my gifts and my blessings. I began to draw near to God when I was folding laundry, going for walks, while I was running, and while I was singing. I made uplifting songs my prayers. I would share with Him what I was thinking. I started to pray this simple prayer over and over, "God, open my eyes to see, open my ears to hear, open my heart to know what Your plan is for my life. Thank You." By simply drawing near to Him, He started to work in my life.

He brought people into my life when I needed someone to speak truth. He gave me courage and strength to make difficult, life-changing decisions. We began walking together; the gap between God and me slowly got smaller and the gap between the world and me started to get wider.

God was becoming more to me than church and rules; He was becoming my guide, provider, and supplier. I was turning toward

Him for direction, instead of toward myself. With belief and confidence I was discovering truth, and for the first time in my life, experiencing love through the Grace offered through His Son, Jesus Christ. I started to love myself and this allowed me to receive love from God.

I had thought that I'd believed that God loved me for many years, but until I truly was able to work through my own unforgiving attitude towards myself, I wasn't able to embrace the depth of how much He delighted in me, His beloved daughter.

Drawing near to God led me to seek Him first and as I leaned into Him so simply, I discovered I needed to understand Him more. He gave me the desire to dig into His Word.

I had based my Christian life up to that point on the sermons I had heard. I had allowed a weekly sermon to be my interpretation of the Bible. I heard an analogy and a light bulb went off in my head: "Standing in a garage doesn't make you a car any more than going to church makes you a Christian." I agreed! That's when I picked up the Bible and started to read it every day. I had such a burning desire to know who God was, that I couldn't stop. In 30 short days, He was transforming my life. He revealed Himself to me through relationships, through my children, even through my finances.

He gave me the strength to work these steps and to implement them into my life. His word made sense to me. I started to fall in love with Him and to understand how much He loved me. Getting to know Him firsthand and personally through His Word, transformed Him in my heart from viewing Him only as my provider, guide, and supplier to Him being my father, my daddy, and my best friend. This, to me, is what it means to have accepted Jesus into my heart.

Here's an elementary explanation of what I've come to realize. We are all children of God and He ultimately wants a relationship with each of us. He sent His son Jesus Christ to live amongst us, to set an example for us of how to live our lives. He spoke truth, demonstrated perfect character, and taught us spiritual principles. He showed us how to connect and have a relationship with our Father, God. Jesus was crucified and triumphed over death. To invite Jesus Christ into my heart means to accept Jesus' way of life; to understand and accept the teachings of Jesus and make every effort to practice His spiritual principles in every area of my daily life.

My faith journey; it's a journey that I walk every day, hand in hand with my Higher Power, My Father God, My King of Kings, My Lord of Lords – my daddy.

He lovingly and compassionately continues to refine me, because I screw up and make mistakes every day; I am a sinner. He patiently works with me as I put pieces of my life together and grow. I still don't attend a church on a regular basis; He hasn't led me to a specific place yet and I don't know if He ever will. I still have not been baptized; but He's giving me the desire, and I might do that soon. What He has done is to heal me from the lingering effects of the Nevers I've experienced in my life. What He has given to me is a peace that passes all understanding, even when I'm in the eye of a hurricane. What He continues to do is to love me and accept me, just as I am. He continues to give me grace and mercy every morning. Nothing that I do will make Him love me more, and nothing that I do will make Him love me less. He has restored me to sanity. He is my "good-enough-ness."

What is your faith journey? What do you believe? Who will restore you from your fallen place? Who will calm your storm? Who will heal your soul wounds? What truth are you seeking?

If you are anything like me, then most likely your plan isn't working. You can fix things and make things better, but only up to a point. At best, it's a temporary fix that won't hold up over the long term.

This is your time. Can you pick up the faith tool to help you garden your life? Take down your opinions and judgments that I had asked you to shelve at the beginning of this chapter, and sincerely consider what step you will take next.

If the tool of faith is one which you have tried before and it didn't seem to work for you, try again with a new point of view. Just draw a little closer to God, and lean on Him a little more. You may be surprised at the results.

If you have never had exposure to the idea of believing in God as your Higher Power, then take a few moments and ask his son, Jesus, to come into your heart and help you with your life, because you have realized you can't fix it yourself. We can't do it all and we weren't meant to. God is there for you – you just have to call out to Him.

Keeping it Personal

1. How is your faith? Where is your faith? Who/what has your confidence?

2. Is there a blockage between you and God? What is keeping you from experiencing Him? What actions do you need to take to restore fellowship – clear, uninhibited fellowship – with Him?

3. God is there. He's never left your side, no matter how many "do's and don'ts" there are between you. What "criteria" do you need to let go, in order for you to experience all of Him?

4. God loves you. He delights in you. Have you accepted Him? Have you allowed Him into your life? If you simply are willing, He will do the rest.

5. Is God your "good-enough-ness?" Stop trying to be good enough. Allow Him to complete you and His grace to cover you.

CHAPTER 4

SURRENDER

STEP 3:

Made a decision to turn our will and our lives over to
the care of God as we understood Him.

MY TOOL:

I am convinced that I need to lay down my will, my pride,
my selfishness, my life DAILY (sometimes many times
throughout the day) and allow God to take care of me.

"The harder you work, the harder it is to surrender."
—Vince Lombardi

Faith brings us to surrender. There is a decision to be made: Will you surrender your will and turn your life over to God? This is our next step to get to a healthier place, to overcoming the Nevers. What does this mean, really, to turn over my will and my life? To surrender is to give up, or resign yourself to something. Your will is the power of choosing your actions; your wish, your determination. Combine these two definitions, and you've got, "give up yourself."

You may be asking the question, *is this for me?* Before you decide, let's explore a little further.

This is a hard one, yes. But all of us are surrendered to something. What we surrender ourselves to ultimately becomes our god; what we worship, turn to, or rely upon. The question is, what are we surrendered to? Is it something firm, solid and long-lasting, or something that can slip away, burn to ashes, or be swallowed?

I discovered I had been surrendered to the opinions of others. I would allow others to dictate how I felt and to influence my decisions; my principles were not firm and solid.

I was surrendered to alcohol. I relied on something that I swallowed to bring me comfort. I was surrendered to relying upon others to meet my needs. I worried constantly about what others were doing to ensure that I got certain results, leading to control and manipulation. But people slip away.

I was surrendered to my own will. I relied upon myself to make everyone happy, to please others, and to figure out what direction

I should take in life. But I ran out of ideas and the well dried up. I was turning to and worshipping unreliable things. False gods lead nowhere but to false ends.

Is having other "gods" before God breaking one of the Ten Commandments? The Bible says in Exodus 20:3 NIV, "You shall have no other gods before me."

We were created from nothingness, given our very breath from our Creator. There is only one solid, reliable source to which we can surrender; our Creator, Father, God. How can we be so prideful to think that we know what's best for our lives, and have confidence that our ways are the right ways? Our brains are finite; we are only capable of seeing what is here and now, our immediate surroundings.

He, on the other hand, is infinite. He knows everyone's thoughts before they think them. We can't change yesterday. We have no idea what's going to happen today, tomorrow, or in the next second. When we operate relying upon our own will, going our own path and direction, we are discounting and essentially eliminating the plan God has for us: His purpose, His will for our life.

We've got no basis for pride. The truth is I am here because God made me. I have gifts and talents because God gave them to me. With Him, I have purpose. Without Him, I am sending Him a message that I know better than He, and I am neglecting His design and purpose for me.

What does that mean, to turn our will over to God? It means going to Him first; with everything in our life; every decision, every reaction, every question, every need. When we decide to live surrendered, we continually need to ask ourselves these three questions:

1. Whose opinion matters?
2. What truth am I seeking?
3. Who is my audience?

The answer to all three of these questions is God. He is our 911 call. Our calling, our goal, is to pursue His will and His approval, because His truth is solid.

This has been one of the biggest changes I've had to make in my life; allowing God to be my 911. When I'm having a bad day, when I have hurt feelings or if things aren't going my way, if I'm frustrated or angry, instead of calling a friend and complaining, I have surrendered to prayer. It doesn't happen in every situation. I am not perfect. But it is my desire, and I do my best.

> *"Seek first His kingdom and His righteousness, and all these things will be given to you as well."*
>
> —MATTHEW 6:33

When I'm in a situation in which I need clarity, or I want to vent, or I am looking for answers, and I feel the need to talk to somebody else before I talk to God, that's showing me that I'm operating out of fear, because I want somebody to know my side of the story. What I'm really seeking at that point is affirmation, or for somebody to just say, "Oh, my. You don't deserve that." When that happens, I'm reverting back to my old behaviors, and putting the approval of others before God's approval.

Don't get me wrong; I believe that God brings people into our life for many reasons. We should connect with others, share our lives, and be honest and transparent about where we are. It's wise to seek counsel from others who we respect, who are like-minded and can support us, love us, and provide us with accountability. But living in surrender means going to them second, not first.

To surrender also means being selfless, not selfish. Our human, sinful nature makes implementing this tool really hard, as consistent surrender is something we will never master in our lifetimes. I believe that I will never get to the point where I can say I'm totally surrendered all day, every day. This step, the surrender tool, is about deciding, having the desire, and pursuing surrender.

This is a process, not something that just happens overnight because we've made the decision. We have to be intentional about surrender and work towards it. We can have the strength one day to let go and give it over to God and the next day grab hold of it again. This becomes something we must do consistently, many times throughout each day. I've experienced the cycle, minute by minute. Let me explain.

Often times, if I'm disturbed by another person's behavior, I can whisper a prayer of surrender. I can ask God to remove from me my expectations, and ask for His will to be done. Then, a few minutes later, my phone rings. The person calling is the person I just "surrendered." Here it is; as we talk, I feel the storm again, I grab hold of my needs, what I want, what I expect – and all of a sudden, I am un-surrendered.

When we pick up whatever it is that we've surrendered, at some point we will start to believe old lies again, try to run life on our own again, or feel the same old emotional storms. It's just a matter of time.

I shared several areas in my life in which I discovered I had been un-surrendered. There could be a list of 20 things we need to surrender, and everyone's list is different. It's not a question of what to surrender and what not to. It's whether or not we're going to surrender at all.

It's black and white. God is, or He is not. Either I am going to surrender to God and what His plan is, or I'm not going to surrender to God and His plan. We cannot straddle the fence. Once we surrender our mind to Him completely, He will take care of us in every way.

Why is it that we might hesitate to turn over our will and our life to God?

Many people have been terribly wounded by others whom they trusted to take care of them. As innocent children, we are forced to rely upon the people God puts into our life to take care of us. If those people hurt us, we might question God's love for us; "If God loved me, how could he allow me to get hurt?" I do not know the answer to this question, or why we are "dealt" the cards that we are. But as adults we get to decide who and how to rely on things and others. The lie is that these are just the cards that we have been dealt. The truth is, you can get a new deck every day.

> *"The faithful love of the Lord never ends! His mercies never cease. Great is His faithfulness; His mercies begin afresh each morning."*
>
> —LAMENTATIONS 3:22-23

Not understanding who God is, prevents people from seeing how much He truly cares for us, how important our needs are to Him and how greatly He loves us. This lack of understanding keeps us from trusting Him and causes us to turn instead to trust ourselves and/or others more.

We tend to trust ourselves, and those around us, more than we trust God. But in fact, our providers are merely channels to the one true Source. How many things do you rely upon as your "source" to meet your needs? Your employer, your spouse, your friendships, your house, the economy, the government, the stock market? When one of these sources fails or dries up, then what happens? Panic. Fear. Anxiety. Worry. Bitterness.

What would it take for you to rely upon the One True Source, God, to meet your needs and to see these other things as channels through which your Source is blessing you? Would it matter if the channels went away? Wouldn't the Source bless you via another channel?

Our blockages – fear, self-reliance, false gods – all separate us from God. As the blockages are removed, we can come into true alignment with Him and His will for our lives. Getting past the "yeah buts," like, "Yeah, but you, God, don't care for me – look at the home I was born into, I was neglected and abused. If you really cared for me, that wouldn't have happened." Getting answers to the "yeah buts," hearing the truth and actually accepting the truth into our heart allows us to surrender.

What does it feel like to surrender?

Surrender feels so freeing. And at the same time, it's frightening because it's not what we're used to. It kind of feels like a homecoming, like you're getting a big hug from someone you care about, having the words whispered in your ear, "It's going to be all right. You're okay. Let me do the work now so you don't have to."

God is the perfect gentleman. He is considerate enough to not jump in our way when we take control and when we think we've got it all figured out. He patiently sits in the corner waiting for us to say, "Hey, it's your turn." He looks at what we've done during the course of our life and says very lovingly, "It's okay. I understand why you did what you did, and I still love you. But you might experience some pain because there are always consequences for behavior. I accept you just as you are. You're okay. I will clean up your mess. I can restore you." In my eyes, He is the perfect father.

When we start to identify our storm, or our discontent or our irritability at the beginning, those feelings are going to occur frequently, because that's how we've operated. When they do occur, instead of responding to them as we would have in the past, we need to simply just take a step back and say, "Okay, God, you know what? I'm surrendering. What is Your will in this situation? Not my will, but Your will." As I said before, this voluntary, conscious act of surrendering may have to happen many times throughout the day, especially as we interact with other people, if we're on a job that's not necessarily where we want to be, or if we're in a relationship that has become unhealthy.

Living surrendered doesn't mean that you have to flee from conflict. It means turning to God about your situation, and then taking a look in the mirror, asking God to help you figure out what you can do to change yourself and have a better approach, or to reset your boundaries. And at some point, you might need to make some changes, whether it's a job or a relationship, or not putting yourself in a vulnerable position with a person that could harm you. That's where you have to use your best judgment.

But in this instant, we need to again tap into our acceptance and peek in the cycle and be clear on how we are using our tools: I am willing. I accept. I have faith, and I surrender.

In Chapter Two, we came to realize that we couldn't do it on our own; that's acceptance. In Chapter Three, we came to believe that God could restore us. Having faith and the belief that God can restore us, do we believe that He can do this completely? This question is so fundamentally important that it needs to be asked again: Do we believe that He can do this completely? If your answer is *yes*, then you've made your decision to surrender your will. "Completely" includes the things that you want, all of your being, including your will.

You have to decide whether or not you trust God to take over, to admit, "I can't do this on my own, here I am. I'm laying my will down. I'm surrendering. I'm waving the white flag; I've accepted life on life's terms. I choose to walk away from my rights and my expectations of how I perceive things to play out." You can solidify the decision by saying this simple prayer:

Dear God. I choose You to be my One true Source. I'm sorry for trying to live this life my way, and for the many wrong choices I've made, please forgive me. Thank you for accepting me and loving me just as I am. I surrender my will and my life, all of me, to You. Open my eyes to see, open my ears to hear, open my heart to know what your plans are for me. Remove anything from me that keeps me from You. Thank You, Father, for Your loving provision over my life. Fill me with Your love and Your Spirit, that I may have the strength each day to live out Your purpose. Amen.

"Ask and it will be given to you; seek and you will find; knock and the door will be opened to you. For everyone who asks receives; the one who seeks finds; and to the one who knocks, the door will be opened." Matthew 7:7-8

With God as our Source, He will give us courage, the courage we need to move forward and through the next steps.

Keeping it Personal

1. What approval do you seek? By whose standards do you live?

2. In the previous chapter, we evaluated where our faith should be placed. If you have placed your faith and trust in your Creator, God, does that trust include His plan for your life? Are you willing to give Him the reins?

3. Are you in awe of a human audience? Who is your audience meant to be? What can you do to ensure your desire toward an audience of ONE?

4. Can you recall a time or a situation that you consciously surrendered to the will of God? How did it turn out? Can you trust Him again?

5. What is holding you back from surrendering completely? Remember, it's a daily decision. How can you live completely surrendered today?

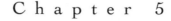

Chapter 5

COURAGE

STEP 4:
Made a searching and fearless moral inventory of ourselves.

MY TOOL:
I need to peel back the layers of who I REALLY am, dig deep and get to the root of my anger, resentments, frustrations, fears, judgments, and ideas. I want to discover the truth about my gifts, my purpose and my strengths.

"Confront the dark parts of yourself, and work to banish them with illumination and forgiveness. Your willingness to wrestle with your demons will cause your angels to sing. Use the pain as fuel, as a reminder of your strength."

—AUGUST WILSON

This chapter is one that might make you want to close this book. Looking inside ourselves is extremely hard work, and can be very painful. There could potentially be doors in your life that have been closed tightly or boarded up for a very long time, or corners of your mind that have collected inches of dust. Going to these places takes willingness, the ability to take an honest look in the mirror, and courage.

We cannot overcome an issue or a problem in our life if we do not know that it exists; we need to search. We cannot become who we were created to be, without embracing our strengths and uncovering our God-given gifts and talents. So we need to look through our lives carefully, in order to find these answers. We need to go back and examine our life up until this point, in order to discover or find that which has been concealed. Searching is looking beyond the superficial aspects of ourselves to discover a motive, reaction, feeling, or basic truth.

How do we do this? Without fear; with courage, boldness, and bravery. We do this with grace and compassion. We do this in faith to discover the truth; the truth will set us free. It is not enough to simply surrender. We must take action with the courage that God gives us through our faith to do this work. If we do not take action by working this step, we risk reverting back to our old behavior patterns of self-reliance and non-surrender. I personally could not let that happen.

I maintained an attitude of willingness. I still had the desire in my heart to become who God created me to be and to move forward. Looking at the sources of all of my open wounds was essential for growth. Equally important was discovering my gifts, identifying the qualities that I liked about myself, my strengths, and my purpose. I believe that If I'm not moving forward and taking action to improve my life on a spiritual or emotional basis, then I'm either getting stale (and stale is stinky and gross), or I'm going backwards. Going backwards was not and is not an option for me. I refuse to forget my bottoming out. I refuse to forget the pain, and I was determined not to lose the ground that I had gained on my journey.

I can remember the day like it was yesterday. I still have the notebook in which I wrote my initial inventory list, and the key word here is "initial"; remember that these steps are intended to be a road map for living, not something that we do just one time. I sat on my bed, pen in hand staring at a blank piece of paper and I started to cry.

I wanted freedom, but I didn't want to go there. I was willing, but I didn't know where to start. There was so much to write, so many wounds, so much pain, so much work. It would've been easy for me not to do it; after all it's my journey, and I can do what I want, right?

But I had invited accountability into my life; I had a friend who was holding my hand as I traveled this road, this "boot camp" through the 12 Steps. She said, "Don't come out of your bedroom until you're done."

That could be a very long time, I thought as I walked humbly to my room. I summoned her back to my room after 15 minutes of tears and random thoughts. I shared with her, "I can't do this, it's too hard – I could fill up this 3-subject spiral notebook and I don't know where to start."

She lovingly and simply said, "Just pray – God will show you – then just write. You can do this."

So with that, I prayed, "Father, remove my fear and show me what you want me to see. Give me strength, direct my thoughts. Thank you for the freedom that is found in truth. Amen." Then, I wrote. It just flowed out of me; it was the start to identifying the blockage that separated me from God, His purpose and His plan for me. Freedom came from simply getting it out, looking at it, and feeling the weight lift off my shoulders. As I flipped back and reviewed what I had written, I smiled. It was right there in front of me, in black and white; I could see what I was dealing with. That alone brought me closer to clarity and inspired my desire to move forward.

What are we looking for? A moral inventory of ourselves; good and bad, right and wrong, negative and positive. This is essentially an accounting, a summary of who we are morally, and what makes us who we are. Our morals are our personal principles and standards. They are reflected by our conduct and behavior. Included in this, we must list things that have been done to us that have impacted us morally. Our fearless inventory is a written list of our life's key events; it's our story, our autobiography.

You might be asking these questions:

Why do I need to go back to this? I cannot change the past, so what's the point? You're right, we cannot change the past, but we can learn from it and discover how the past has affected how we currently live and feel. Our past inventory also sheds light on and brings awareness to deep-rooted weeds that choke out truth, and contaminate how we think about ourselves and how we view others and life situations. Having the courage to go to this place allows God to garden our lives.

Why do I need to write this down? I don't like to write. Why can't I just do the correct thing, moving forward?

Because it doesn't work that way. How many times have you reflected on something that you've done, thought about it, and vowed to do it differently next time – and then that next time comes, and you do the same thing over again? I know that I've circled the same mountains hundreds of times because my thoughts didn't turn into action. When we put things in writing, when we can look at something and see it in black and white, read it – it becomes more than a thought. Making a list is taking action. Writing is a form of commitment; it takes time, intentional thought, and work.

Where there is darkness there is no healing. Our thoughts can get left in the dark. If you are serious about your emotional and spiritual growth, if you desire more from life than what you're currently experiencing, you need to take your inventory in writing.

Successful businesses spend thousands of dollars and many months, maybe years, conducting critical business inventories or evaluations. Why? To improve the quality of their business. Doesn't it make sense to conduct a regular evaluation of our lives, in order to improve the quality of our lives? Unfortunately, most people don't take the time to do this. Many simply do not want to. And others don't know where or how to start. That was me, for the majority of my life. I wasn't aware that I should do this myself. I wasn't taught this tool.

But just as any well-run company takes a regular written inventory to identify what products or parts they have on hand, what's gained and lost, what the value is on each product and part – we must, too. All by itself, this step holds priceless value in revealing to you exactly where you are and why.

The comforting truth about making this inventory list is that God will meet us where we are. He knows that we are not perfect. He knew, before we knew, what we were going to say and do and think, and how we would respond to every experience, every situation, every Never.

> *"O Lord, you have examined my heart and know everything about me. You know when I sit down or stand up. You know my thoughts even when I'm far away. You see me when I travel and when I rest at home. You know everything I do. You know what I am going to say even before I say it."*
>
> —PSALM 139:1-4

This is a journey, not a race. The inventory process is not about how quickly we can wipe our slate clean and forget about this. As we simply start and ask for His guidance, He makes it known to us through our thoughts, through our experiences and through others, what we need to work through. He lovingly reveals to us what is blocking us from experiencing true freedom and joy in our hearts, and what is blocking us from experiencing a personal, loving relationship with Him.

We do not have to do anything with our inventory right away, only when we are ready, willing, and led by God. We don't need to send letters to people on our list who we have harmed or who have wounded us. In Chapter Six, we learn our next tool, the next step. There, we will take appropriate action with our inventory, but right now, be fully where you are at this moment – don't look ahead. This is your time to reflect, you're moving forward to start the restoration process to become whole, discover truth, and heal.

How do you go about identifying behaviors and judgments that need to be changed?

God will reveal these things to us as we do this work continuously, and ask Him to open our eyes to see. Sometimes our external behaviors and judgments are the last things to go. As we grow spiritually and connect with God, He shows us the weeds in our garden, we change from the inside, our hearts heal, our thinking aligns with our Creator's, and our lives become newly fruitful.

One of the challenges I've had to overcome is the temptation to pass judgment on others. I didn't see that I was judgmental. In fact, I truly believed I was the least judgmental person I knew, and I would get frustrated with others who I felt were passing judgment on me. Because I was unaware of this attitude or spirit within me, I was not seeking for God to help me in this area. I did not pray specifically asking Him to help me be less judgmental and more accepting of others. This was a weed in my life that God had to reveal to me: He compassionately showed me how my thoughts, words, and facial expressions towards others at times were inappropriate. The very thing I thought others were doing towards me, I was projecting onto others. He lifted the blinders off my eyes so that I could see this. With this awareness, and through my growth, I've become a lot more accepting, patient, and tolerant of others, to a degree that I would have found shocking before. I look at a person who maybe isn't "living life" the way that I would, and now I feel compassion and love in my heart instead of judgment. I have a desire to learn more, to seek to understand, and to listen.

Before I became more aware, I'm embarrassed to admit that I would often think, "Wow, I would never do what they're doing. I can't believe it. They are wrong. I am better. That is not okay." Unfortunately, that was my pattern of thinking for most of my life.

I've experienced many challenges, obstacles, and Nevers in my life and as I worked through them by implementing this tool into my life, I've become less judgmental. I've become more loving, more understanding, and more compassionate. Don't get me wrong – once in a while I'll still walk in a room and size somebody up by what she's wearing. But now, I am aware of this and can quickly change my thoughts and attitude – because I want to. I want to look inside myself, to understand why I might be projecting that attitude, and to address head on with myself what I discover. God is still refining me in this area. But He has given me a new set of glasses through which I see others and myself.

By unpacking my life and taking my moral inventory, I've overcome many fears and insecurities, which were deep-rooted weeds that contributed to me passing judgment on others. This tool reveals truth, which allows us to love who we are, accept who we are, and have confidence through awareness and knowledge of our strengths.

Do you need to bring others into this process?

It is not necessary to bring others into this inventory process. Actually, I would recommend to you that this be used as a time of personal reflection, with one exception which I will explain in a minute. If we have other people taking our inventory, we become defensive, and this can be more destructive than productive. God will not give us more than we can handle and process at any one time. When we are ready to deal with certain things, that's when it is time. Just because someone else sees something that may not be right in your life, doesn't mean that you're ready to deal with it or go through it.

Only when we are at a place of conviction can a heartfelt change be made. It will not happen on another person's timetable. This process is more about the condition of our heart, and what our head knows. An objective approach is our head deciding what we should or shouldn't do, and our heart is about our feelings, surroundings, experiences, and situations.

As we search deep to start our list, we need to tap into our feelings. Our thoughts will lead us towards our feelings, and those are the things which we write down. The list can be as short or as long as it needs to be. There's not a right or a wrong way.

My list initially was short, and as I continue to live this and use this tool, there are more things that are added onto it. A lot of things have gotten crossed off as I've worked through them. But I can tell you that just a couple months ago, there were more items added to my list. Our goal is progress, not perfection.

Here's the exception. Remember, we are looking for a moral inventory which consists of good and bad, positive and negative. For many of us, because we've been so wounded and have experienced many Nevers, we have a difficult time recognizing any claim to moral high ground in ourselves. We have a hard time seeing our strengths, our positives, the things that we do right – our good character qualities. This is where we might need some help, and can invite others to point out positive qualities that we have.

I needed help. I was asked to make this list while I was in treatment. It was part of a self-esteem building assignment that I had to do and share with a group. When I sat down to make my list of "assets" I numbered a piece of paper 1 to 10 in two areas, character and physical. Then I sat, staring at the paper and racking my brain just to write something positive. I started with character assets:

1. Great listener
2. Honest
3. Compassionate
4. Hard worker/Strong work ethic
5. Smart

Those were all that I could come up with, so I switched to physical assets. I could not think of anything. I was carrying around so many lingering after-effects from my Nevers that all I saw were my faults. When I looked into the mirror in the morning, I hated who I saw, so to write anything positive about myself physically was extremely challenging for me. When it was my turn to present my assignment to my small group I started to weep. I shared what I came up with and they helped me fill in the blanks. Character assets continued:

6. Patient
7. Faithful
8. Organized
9. Real with self and others, and brings out the "real" in others
10. Trust builder (Trustworthy; builds trust in others)

Physical assets:
1. Smile
2. Beautiful eyes
3. High cheekbones
4. Naturally beautiful
5. Warm/Olive skin color
6. Long hair – thick/straight/full
7. Soft hands

8. Strong
9. Endurance
10. (I didn't write anything down at the time for #10…just being honest!)

Admittedly, this was hard for me to hear. I didn't believe most of what these women were saying about me, but what I was asked to do next is speak them out loud saying, "I am…" or "I have a…" With 10 sets of eyes on me I started to speak truth into my life about who I was, out loud for the very first time in many years. "I am a great listener, I am honest, I am compassionate, I am a hard worker with strong work ethic, I am smart, I am patient, I am faithful." My voice got louder and more confident as I completed the list, believing it more at the end than I had when I started.

I wanted to share this with you, because these were positives about who I was, and who I am. I just needed help from others to allow me to see them. Today I believe these things and more – I'm embracing my gifts and my strengths – but I had to start somewhere. This was my start, and it can be yours, too. Bring others into the equation to help you see the truth about who you are, and to affirm your positive characteristics.

My hope is that you have the courage to implement this tool into your life. My desire for you is that you are still willing to move forward. Are you ready? If so, I have some resources that you can tap into to help you. Visit my website **overcomingthenevers.com/ tools.** There, you can download free memory stimulation guides and worksheets that show you how to work this step.

The promises written in the book *Alcoholics Anonymous* started to manifest in my life as I worked this step and implemented it into my life; they are available for you too:

"If we are painstaking about this phase of our development, we will be amazed before we are halfway through. We are going to know a new freedom and a new happiness. We will not regret the past nor wish to shut the door on it. We will comprehend the word serenity and we will know peace. No matter how far down the scale we have gone, we will see how our experience can benefit others. That feeling of uselessness and self-pity will disappear. We will lose interest in selfish things and gain interest in our fellows. Self-seeking will slip away. Our whole attitude and outlook upon life will change. Fear of people and of economic insecurity will leave us. We will intuitively know how to handle situations which used to baffle us. We will suddenly realize that God is doing for us what we could not do for ourselves. Are these extravagant promises? We think not. They are being fulfilled among us—sometimes quickly, sometimes slowly. They will always materialize if we work for them."[1]

If we work for them. Courage is strength.

---

1 AA Services, *The Big Book,* (AA World Services, 2001, 4th Edition), pp. 83-84

Keeping it Personal

1. Have you asked God to guide you and reveal to you what you need to write?

2. What's keeping you from writing? From acknowledging? From accepting?

3. How can you "be fully where you are" TODAY?

4. What are you projecting?

5. Are you noticing faults in others more readily because that same fault is in your life?

Chapter 6

ADMISSION

STEP 5:

Admitted to God, to ourselves, and to another human
being the exact nature of our wrongs.

MY TOOL:

I speak my life story out loud to God, myself, to someone I trust. I confess and
take responsibility for my wrongs and I share my strengths and my gifts.

*"One of the hardest things in this world is to admit
you are wrong. And nothing is more helpful in
resolving a situation than its frank admission."*

— BENJAMIN DISRAELI

Here we are with our written moral inventory. We've searched, looked in the mirror and identified who we are morally, or at least we've started. We see it in black and white, the good and the bad. So, what's next? We must share. Speak it. Give it a name. Own it.

At first, this tool can seem terrifying or frightening. I know that it was, for me. Not so much with sharing my positive attributes, those things that others helped me to realize, but in sharing the negative parts of who I was; my garbage, the junk in my closet, my ickiness. Are you kidding me? – that's scary. Just the thought of sharing all that I had written down gave me anxiety and a very large knot in my stomach. I had secrets, some not-so-pretty private thoughts, and a lot of darkness in my personal inventory notebook, much of which I had never bestowed upon another.

The thoughts racing through my mind were, "What in the world will she think of me after I tell her this? Am I bad? Am I a loser? Will she still accept me, will she still like me? Will I be rejected and judged?" I also thought, "Maybe I will just pick and choose what I share from my inventory with her, another human being, and keep the really shameful, embarrassing things between God and myself." I had more fear about verbalizing my morality with another imperfect person than I did with God, who is perfect.

Valuing the opinions of others, and focusing on the measuring stick the world offers, can be a roadblock to admitting our darkest secrets. Withholding what I had discovered out of fear was dishonest, which is wrong, so I let that thought pass on by. Additionally, I had spent my whole life wronging my Creator, so what would stop me from continuing down that same path in the future? I needed to do something different to experience different results.

The contemplation and feelings were very real, but I could not let them prevent me from continuing on. I was still willing. I was committed to continue walking with God in faith. I had courage. I desperately wanted freedom – do you? If so, keep putting one foot in front of the other and implement this tool into your life.

There are two things that happen when we admit. First, admitting is taking action; it is confessing and acknowledging. We cannot change what we do not acknowledge, and without change there is no moving forward, no doing things differently. Confession breaks down barriers and removes the blockage which keeps us from experiencing God.

There is cleansing, a washing away, and the start of restoration, when we confess. As we walk in honesty and in truth, we start the reconciliation process with ourselves, with God, and with others. Moving into the light gradually bridges the gap between God and us, and between ourselves and others, which results in cultivating peace and harmony. Need I say more? Isn't that what we are all looking for? Freedom, serenity, and tranquility.

Each time we reveal our immorality, we are speaking out of who we are; our soul, mind, will, and emotions. When we confess, we are looking for understanding, love and compassion. We are social beings who need and long for connection, community, and acceptance. That is why there is significant growth with this, too; sharing with another human being, someone who understands.

Second, to "admit" is to allow to enter, to grant entrance. We are saying *yes, open this door.* We are inviting in accountability and allowing others into our world. It's so easy to shy away from account-ability. It's a vulnerable place to be, and it's not always pleasant to have someone to whom we must answer, someone who knows what we are up to. When we invite this in through admitting, we will be held to a higher standard, one that will allow us to reap unbelievable benefits in our lives; we must remain willing.

Without accountability, we can talk ourselves out of taking action, get sidetracked into losing focus, and fall off the wagon, reverting back to our old ways. If we can embrace healthy account-ability and be deliberate about pressing forward with it, our world will change significantly for the better.

I love the way this quote is written:

"Accountability breeds response-ability." —Stephen R. Covey

He hyphenates the word "responsibility" because it is two-fold. "Response" is an answer or reply, in words or through action. "Ability" is the power or capacity to do or act; physically, mentally, legally, morally, financially, etc. How or what will we do, and do we have the strength, courage, and willingness to do it? We have a "response-ability" for ourselves, in all areas of our lives, in all of our roles. No one can attempt to change us or to control us, unless we give them the power. We need to be the change. Period. Admitting opens this door. Will you walk through it?

Accountability has been the backbone of my spiritual and emotional growth. I know I would not be where I am today without it. Admitting I was an alcoholic. Calling it out. Giving it a name. Owning it. I acknowledged it and shared it with God and someone whom I trusted, another human being. When I did that, I instantly invited in accountability, which held me to "response-ability." I knew what I had to do, I knew what action I needed to take, and with the strength God gave me I was able to respond. I haven't always enjoyed having the accountability I've invited, but without it, I know where I would be; back to where I was, or lower.

What are wrongs? Let's cut to the chase, not sugar-coat it, and call a spade a spade. Wrongs are sin. Yes, they are. Our wrongs can damage, harm, violate, take advantage of, mistreat, and offend. Sin is more than just "breaking the rules." Sin is immoral action. It can be anger, lust, envy, jealousy, pride, the failure to grow. Sin is the failure to respond to the love of God. Sin is condemnation of self and others. Sin is disobedience. Sin destroys us from the inside; it is toxic – because sin separates us from God. God hates sin.

> *"If we don't change, we don't grow. If we don't grow, we are not really living. Growth demands a temporary surrender of security."*
>
> —GAIL SHEEHY

Wrong thinking can also prevent us from experiencing joy and being fully alive. When we decide that something is true, that "truth" adheres to us, even if it's false. Believing messages about who you are that are simply not true, is wrong.

Remember, our fearless inventory is a written list of our life. It's our story, our biography. We took note of what we've done morally, but we also included things that have happened morally towards us. This is where the lies creep in, the false "truths." The only way to overcome the lingering after-effects of our Nevers is to shine light into what we believe. When we share these core thoughts and beliefs with another human being, we have another voice, another perspective to consider.

Have you ever written a letter, proofed it a dozen times, and prior to it being signed, sealed, and delivered, invited another person to check it over for mistakes? You were most likely confident it was ready to go out the door, but having another set of eyes give it a once-over revealed a few typos and grammar errors. Surprised at the findings, since you'd been certain it was flawless, you had to incorporate change.

This happens to all of us. When we look at something long enough, we have a hard time seeing things that are wrong. Things get overlooked and become normal or customary; they become our "truth." Unfortunately our "truth" might be wrong. We might believe the lies. We need to invite another set of eyes into our lives to gain insight and be willing to see and hear ourselves from a different angle. The lies are usually concealed, unseen enemies that flourish if left unchecked.

Let me share with you how easily these lies and untruths, can manifest in our lives. When I was born, I was the youngest of three, the baby in our family. My sister was six years older than me and was developing friendships with other little girls and playing, living age-appropriately. My brother was two years older than me. He wasn't in school yet, but my mom had developed friendships with other moms who had little boys, so he spent a lot of time playing, wrestling, and doing what boys do.

I know that I was a welcome member of our family. I had a loving, nurturing mother and a father who adored me. I'm sure I was the little baby sister who received a whole lot of attention for the first few years of my life.

As I grew older and started to toddle around, I can remember being around adults most often; going places with my mom, spending time with her friends as well as with my grandparents. I wanted to play with other kids, but unfortunately I didn't have any friends. This is when I became the annoying little sister. I would try to play with my big sister, but I wasn't old enough to do what she was doing, or to understand how to play like she did. I would attempt to play with my brother but I wasn't a boy – I wasn't rough and tough, I couldn't keep up with the cowboys and Indians, so that wasn't an option for me either.

At that tender age somewhere between 3 and 5, before I started kindergarten, I started to believe that I was not good enough, and that in order to be likeable, I needed to be someone else. I believed that if I was older like my sister, then I could have friends. If I was a boy like my brother, then maybe others would like me and I would be accepted. These were my reasons and they made sense to me – how else could I have dealt with the pain of feeling alone and rejected?

As a child, I was unaware that these powerful damaging beliefs would become the foundation of how I operated as an adult. These core lies were evident in my work, in my marriage, and in my relationships with others, myself, and God. It was not okay to be me. I needed to perform or to be someone else to be liked and accepted. I was not good enough.

These seeds of lies were grown in a seemingly healthy environment. Imagine what toxic weed could develop in one's life if there was abuse, physically, verbally or sexually? Or abandonment? What lies do you believe? There are many; let me name a few:

I am bad
I am not a good person
It's not okay to cry
I am dirty

I don't deserve to get attention or to be heard
I'm a failure
I can never do anything right

These beliefs of wrong thinking subsequently drive us to wrong doing. They are equally, if not more, important to confess and dig up, because every external behavior starts first in our thoughts. Changing our thinking will change our lives. It is not our intent to focus on the negative, but by identifying and acknowledging we can overcome, offset what we've realized with truth, and start planting and nurturing new seeds.

With whom, with what human being, do we share the exact nature of our wrongs?

I do not know the answer to this question for you; each person is unique and has different connections. There are many options available to you, but asking God to reveal this person is crucial. Walk in faith, expecting that God will bring somebody into your life. His desire for you is freedom. Prayerfully consider asking God to lead you, but waste no time, take action, and do not put this off. Pursue the answer and work this step – I can tell you that a new happiness and a new peace awaits you.

Let me suggest some options. Consider a counselor, a pastor, or a mentor, someone whom you trust. Maybe there is another person that you know who has gone before you, who may understand your journey, speak truth into your life, and not judge. Most often, this person will not be your spouse, significant other, family member, or best friend. Don't get me wrong – at some point, once you've experienced healing and acceptance from the items on your inventory list, you may feel comfortable sharing more personal details with these people. Find somebody who you can trust who is not emotionally attached to your life.

You could consider hiring a life-coach, one who understands the significance of this work. I see so much progress made in my clients' lives as we move through this step, and I would be thrilled to help anyone experience the freedom that awaits them on the other side.

Or, you could consider joining a 12-step group that you can relate to. Most 12-step groups offer a sponsorship program, and are available to walk with you through the work.

Through my company, Keeping it Personal, we offer a 3-day course which provides a safe enviornment with an unique method of guiding individuals through the process of making a searching and fearless moral inventory and admitting to another human being the exact nature of wrongs. You can learn more about this option at **keepingitpersonal.com/services**.

Admission is confession, an external expression of the internal transformation of conversion that happens in our hearts. Conversion is progress; it is continuous, ongoing, not just a once-in-a-lifetime moment. As we grow along spiritual lines, our wrongs and our sinful desires will lessen. As we continue to walk in the light, discover truth, and come out of the darkness of our past, we heal and fall in love with who we are. This lifelong process brings us ever closer to the holiness and love of God.

The trials in our life are mercies in disguise. This is a commitment to honesty and growth; a commitment to change. You could make an excuse to stay unchanged, to not move, or to wait another day. This tool, we cannot refuse to use – so what do you choose? Become *you*.

Keeping it Personal

1. Why is it difficult for you personally to admit where you have been wrong?

2. Who in your life would you categorize as "someone to answer to"?

3. We've seen that we have "response – ability" – who have you given the power to change you? What can you do to change that?

4. What are you thinking about yourself? About others? About God? Is it true? Why is it true?

5. You've been called to be the change. Do you desire it? What step can you take this second toward becoming you?

CHAPTER 7

TRANSFORMATION

STEP 6:

Were entirely ready to have God remove all these defects of character.

MY TOOL:

I am completely willing to have God change me and
redirect me to become who He created me to be.

"Create in me a clean heart, O God, and renew a right,
persevering, and steadfast spirit within me."

— PSALM 51:10

R efreshed. Having exposed every dark cranny of our past, and having swept out every dusty corner in our lives of which we are aware, we feel grateful for the grace, forgiveness, and acceptance that we've received freely from God and our confessor. Our spiritual beliefs are becoming spiritual experiences. Are you ready to move forward? To continue your walk honestly in the light?

If you are ready, are you entirely ready? Wholly, completely, and unreservedly? As difficult as the previous tools were to pick up and implement, this tool of transformation takes commitment – a lifelong commitment and perseverance towards refining and renewing. This is where the rubber meets the road.

To truly understand the meaning behind the words in this step, we must unpack them. We will do this backwards, starting with character.

Character is what one is; it's our individuality – it's you. You are special, unique, one-of-a-kind; there is no other you. Our appearance, morale, personality, style, temperament, our complete makeup, exists exactly the way it does at this very moment for two reasons.

The first reason is because God created us that way. We were born with certain God-given character traits, hand-picked features that He wanted us to have, internally and externally. For most of us, we can recall our external God-given traits, our appearance, by sifting through baby pictures and those from our younger years. I was born with brown hair, olive-colored skin, and a pointy chin.

My internal character, personality, temperament? I needed to ask my mom about that, so I got her on the phone. She said, "I wanted another baby, and God gave me you!" On reflecting further and trying to provide an answer to my question, which was random and unexpected, she said, "You were a good baby – happy. You were very playful and you loved being around people. You were likeable, personable, compassionate and concerned about others. You were independent. You loved to sing. As you grew up, you became unorganized and messy – keeping a clean room was extremely challenging for you."

In that brief conversation I had with my mom, she shared a broad overview of who I was, a snapshot. We each possess hundreds of character qualities prior to us taking our first breath. Those, we were intended to have: they were divinely placed in us, and the things which make me, me, and you, you.

When God created heaven and earth, light and dark, the water and dry land, He saw it as good. When He let the land produce vegetation and allowed the water and land to teem with living creatures, He saw it as good. But when God created mankind in His own image, "God saw all that He had made, and it was very good." (Genesis 1:31) We were not simply just created good, we were created in a high degree: extremely, exceedingly, precisely, particularly and exactly. We were created very well.

Some of these very good traits will get the nourishment that they need to grow and develop, and some, unfortunately, will not; they will be covered up or dismissed and others will be developed in their places.

Secondly, our role models, environment, and our experiences contribute to our character. Education and development start at a young age. What we see going on in our world early on is what we learn. We observe how our parents, guardians, and teachers interact and respond to life's situations and in relationships. Whether they demonstrate weak or strong, positive or negative characters, these traits are acquired, learned, and passed on. As children, we are greatly influenced by those around us. What we are led to believe and what we see shapes our future and how we operate as adults; it develops character.

A significant role model in my life was my father; one of the most amazing men I know, next to my husband. He is faithful, honest, forgiving, gracious, reliable, and unselfish. I remember asking him frequently as I was growing up, "Dad, did you have a good day today?"

His answer was consistent and always the same, "Ter-bear, every day is a great day." From what I could see as a child, and still to this day, my dad maintains a positive attitude. I know now the reality is that every day had its challenges for him, as it does for all of us.

What he taught me was that happiness is a choice. We can choose each moment of every day to make it a great day, we can choose to focus on our blessings and the positive, or we can choose not to. From this one example, my father demonstrated to me gratefulness, faithfulness, happiness, and decisiveness, all of which add up to positive character.

You've most likely heard the statement, "You are a product of your environment." The message doesn't stop there. W. Clement Stone says, "So choose the environment that will best develop you toward your objective. Analyze your life in terms of its environment. Are the things around you helping you toward success – or are they holding you back?"

As adults, we have the capacity to adjust our surroundings or to do something about our environment; unfortunately, as children, we do not. If the environment we were raised in was unhealthy, abusive and contaminated with negativity, we could develop traits of anger, low-self esteem, negativity, or resentment.

A friend of mine attributes much of her insecurity, and her guarded, suspicious character traits to her experience of being bullied when she was a teenager. She was called names and picked on for many years. Attending school was a challenge and a draining struggle. She constantly worried about how she looked, what she wore, and what she said, but nothing she did was good enough to gain the acceptance of others.

These torturous days and beliefs about who she was, and not good enough have carried into her adult life. She struggles with trusting others, feeling that if someone is nice to her that must mean that they want something from her. Additionally, she is constantly trying to gain approval from others by performing. She is exhausted from jumping through hoops to meet everyone's expectations. She is a people pleaser, and the only person she is not pleasing is herself.

Whether God-given or obtained through our life's journey, we've developed character and have become who we are. All of us come with our own set of negative character traits. We can't help it – it's just the way it is. We know they are there; some stick out like sore thumbs, while others are harder to detect. The truth is, they don't have to stay. We can change the way in which we perceive these negative traits, these defects of character. Instead of having an attitude of *I am who I am and this is how I will be*, we can work towards understanding what the consequences are of keeping our negative traits around and how they influence our lives. When we know what they are and reflect upon them, we can work towards eliminating them, with God's help, and make changes for the better.

One of my defects of character is procrastination. This is no secret; I've wrestled with it for a very long time. Remember, my mom shared that as I grew up, I had become unorganized and messy, that keeping a clean room was extremely challenging for me. Well, it's because this is one of the character traits that had developed in me. I put things off. I find it ironic that "procrastinate" is a verb, which indicates it's an action word, when the word itself means to defer action.

Unfortunately this trait can result in missed opportunities and emotional weariness. Williams James says, "Nothing is so fatiguing as the eternal hanging on of an uncompleted task." When we procrastinate, we are not taking the appropriate action that we know we need to take. We carry thoughts about what we should be doing in our minds. Our thoughts turn into lies and mis-beliefs, and we start to feel that we aren't good enough, or that we have failed, which is self-sabotaging. We carry the stress of the unfinished business on our shoulders, which drains us and holds us back.

How do I know this? Because I'm experiencing the effects of procrastination through the writing of this book. It is staring me in the face as I type every word of this chapter. There have been many days I've wanted to stop and not move forward. I've pushed back deadlines, rationalized excuses and wasted many good writing days by allowing every distraction to creep into my life.

The tapes that continuously play in my mind are *I am not a writer, I'm in over my head, this is too hard for me.* What I would rather do are the things that I know how to do, like coach a client through a life obstacle or bring individuals through our 3-day course. I would rather do things that are sociable and fun, like visit with a friend over coffee or go to a movie. The last thing I want to be doing is something in which I don't feel confident – something that is extremely hard work – something that is refining me to the core and forcing me to dig deep into the depths of my soul.

Fear is the root of my procrastination. Fear of failure. Fear of what others might think. Fear of judgment. Fear of success; *what happens if this really takes off, what does that look like?* In all the significant areas of my life where I've allowed procrastination to set in, I can see that the core of not taking action is fear.

F.E.A.R is False Evidence Appearing Real. When I am operating in fear, I am not operating in faith. When I am not walking in faith, I am leaving God out of my equation. So the questions I need to ask myself are; where is God? If He has given me this vision and the words to share in this book, why am I allowing my thoughts and untruths to become stumbling blocks?

I've been carrying this project around on my shoulders for many months now, and I've felt stressed out and weary. Determined to persevere, to move forward in obedience to what God has called me to do and write this book, I am choosing to implement this tool now – again – in this area of my life, having a new awareness. I've been shown very clearly what needs to be removed; I believe I know what I can do to work towards eliminating it, with God's help, and make changes for the better. I am entirely ready to have God remove procrastination.

To work this out, I must take action and make some changes. I'm inviting in new forms of accountability, a prayer team of women to support and encourage me, and I'm daily reading an identity statement-prayer that I've written that invites truth into my life. This prayer grounds me, reminds me of who I am in Christ and as a child of God. It's becoming the foundation that I need each morning to set my feet firmly on the ground. This is the prayer that I wrote:

"Father, You are my life, my Creator, my Source, my every-thing. Your focus is my focus. You love me with an everlasting love. My heart is filled with joy and excitement because You, the God of all, are living in me.

Lord, You are my good-enough-ness. Your perfect track record has become my track record – together we are equipped to face every situation. You fill me to overflowing and we are a huge blessing to everyone we encounter. Your light shines through me.

You created me to completely depend upon You. You are my strength. We are successful together. Thank You that we are victorious in everything we do and in every day of our life. You are my protection, safety, and shelter. I am 100% safe and secure in You. Your plans for me are for good.

You accept, love, and approve of me at all times. Your love for me is unchanging. Nothing I do makes You love me more. Nothing I do makes You love me less. There is nothing that You are not capable of and with You in me, we are a winning team.

You are my affirmation, my completeness. You Lord are my audience of One."

I believe it is a gift that I've discovered how this character defect has impacted my life. I am more than ready to have it removed. I know it will take time, and that it will surface again from time to time. But, I will continue to work towards overcoming, and do what it takes to press on.

The next important word in this step that we need to look at is "all," as in all of these defects of character. "All" is every, all kinds, all sorts. "All" is the total whole quantity, not just a fraction or the part that would be easy to remove. "All" is each and every one that God reveals to us, whether we like it or not.

The last word we need to unpack is the first word written in this step: "were." If I could make one suggestion to Bill Wilson, the courageous man who authored the 12 Steps of Alcoholics Anonymous, it would be this. Change the word "Were" to "We are," or "I am."

"Were" implies past tense; something that at one time was, whereas "We are" or "I am" says "now and in the future" – continually. Like each of these steps, they are not steps we take one time; they are steps that we live. At any given time while living these steps, you may discover a "defect of character." When that time comes, will you be entirely ready to have God remove it? Don't answer this question too quickly. Removing things from our lives that we've been hanging on to for decades can be extremely painful. It takes a lot of work and a solid commitment. But it can be done. The rewards for our obedience are priceless and beyond our wildest imagination.

Once the light shines into one of these areas, will you reflect, seek to understand how it is impacting your life, and take action, with God's help, to change? Continued willingness is essential. What you see today or in the coming months will be different from what you see in the coming years. Can you say "I am entirely ready to have God remove all these defects of character"? If your answer is "yes," and I hope it is, let's move forward and take the next step.

Keeping it Personal

1. This transforming process is a lifelong commitment. Are you willing? Why or why not?

2. Take a few minutes to think about you. Perhaps, like Teri, ask a family member or close friend to help. What character traits were you born with (those which God divinely placed in you)?

3. Are there good character traits that you have let fall away? How can you begin to nourish them back into your life?

4. What negative character traits would you like to work toward eliminating in your life?

5. Are you allowing F.E.A.R. to influence you? What does God say about fear? (See Psalm 56:11, Isaiah 41:10, II Timothy 1:7, and 1 John 4:18, just to name a few.)

CHAPTER 8

HUMILITY

STEP 7:
Humbly asked Him to remove our shortcomings.

MY TOOL:
Plainly and apologetically, I pray and ask God to give
me strength to help me where I am weak.

*"What makes humility so desirable is the marvelous thing it does to us;
it creates in us a capacity for the closest possible intimacy with God."*
— MONICA BALDWIN

The idea of transformation can be frightening. Embarking upon anything outside the known or familiar, whether healthy or unhealthy, often creates an inner struggle around separation, change, and having things taken away or removed.

You have answered "yes." You are entirely ready to have God remove all those defects of character, your shortcomings – the objectionable things you discovered about yourself to which you've been clinging. This step gives your "yes" feet. The action itself is very simple; we say a prayer. But the attitude with which we approach the prayer is most important. We humbly ask God, through prayer, to remove our shortcomings. Let's explore our approach, our mental outlook, and our frame of mind, before we ask.

Our initial attitude – what we discussed in Chapter One – is willingness. I cannot express how significant it is for us to maintain an attitude of willingness. It takes willingness to overcome the lingering after-effects of our Nevers and to sustain the progress that we've made. We cannot ever – at any time – take our spiritual and emotional growth lightly.

We need to be intentional about it every day of our lives, searching for truth, knowledge, and understanding. Walking this journey requires our being continuously willing to overcome, refine, and become. If we are not, if we become complacent with this, we will revert back to our old behaviors, our old thinking patterns, our will; it's just a matter of time. Humility is knowing this.

Humility is not being humiliated, put down or embarrassed, although at times we may have these feelings as a result of our behavior. Every action that we take, every word that we speak, every intention or thought that we have, will manifest into something and result in a consequence. Depending on what the cause is, the effect will either be positive or negative. Unfortunately, the negative effects at times result in a painful loss of pride, self-respect, or dignity; humiliation. It is in these moments, if we are willing to see, that we can identify our shortcomings or our character defects that need to be removed.

We are aware of what some of these are right now, based on our personal inventory. But, we are at the beginning – we're just starting to scratch the surface. Living with an attitude of willingness and humility, we will, from time to time, be presented with more attitudes, beliefs, and behaviors that need to be removed, worked out, or healed in our lives.

Humility is the healthiest, most productive state in which to be. It is not proud or arrogant. It's being modest and acknowledging the fact that, alone and apart from our Source, God, we are nothing; we are incapable of change, and incapable of experiencing true freedom. When we are humble, we embrace the feelings of insignificance, inferiority, and subservience. We take ourselves out of the driver's seat, remove ourselves from the throne and surrender to our Higher Power.

Remember in Chapter Four where we picked up our surrender tool with Step Three, "We made a decision to turn our will and our lives over to the care of God as we understood Him." To sincerely implement this tool, humility, we are again turning our will, our lives, our plans, and our egos over to the care of God. We are transferring all control over to Him. We are inviting Him to separate us from what we've uncovered and discovered, what He revealed to us in our lives that is not pleasing to Him; our shortcomings; our character defects. We are asking Him to heal us, restore us, refine us, and transform us.

Another tool which we use as we grow to understand the meaning behind this step is faith. In Chapter Three, we discussed Step Two, "Came to believe that a Power greater than ourselves could restore us to sanity." When we humbly ask God, we are stepping out in faith, into the unknown. We trust that His plans for us are for good, and that, apart from these things that we are about to have removed, we will be okay.

Jeremiah 29:11-13 pulls these steps together beautifully: "For I know the plans I have for you, declares the LORD, plans to prosper you and not to harm you, plans to give you hope and a future. Then you will call on me and come and pray to me, and I will listen to you. You will seek me and find me when you seek me with all your heart."

I didn't know what my life would look like once I "let go of the wheel" allowing God to be my captain, to lead me and guide me. I had reservations in my heart. I questioned in my mind, *do I really want these things removed? If I let go of the anger, resentment and unforgiving, will I be hurt again, or will those people who have wounded me treat me better? What happens if I forgive, change, and move forward, but the people in my life don't? Then what? Will I be viewed as weak or a failure if I surrender?*

Once I stopped the racing thoughts in my mind I realized, *what do I have to lose?* The weight of these burdens had become too heavy for me to bear and I was sick and tired of what I had been doing which wasn't working. So I picked up all my tools, gripped them tightly, and humbly prayed this simple prayer, because, *yes*, I was entirely ready to have God remove all my defects of character. My list at that time was: comparing myself to others, dishonesty with my feelings, the lies I believed (that I'm not good enough, that I'm a failure), narrow-mindedness, fear, insecurity, and selfishness. I was more than ready.

Are you humbly ready to have God remove all your shortcomings? If so, take a moment – speak this prayer.

"Heavenly Father, Thank You for loving me and for accepting me just as I am. Come into all areas of my life. Remove from me all negativity and anything that blocks me from doing Your will and prevents me from being who You created me to be. Open my eyes to see any lie that I have come to believe about myself – and those that prevent me from loving You and others better. Give me strength. Give me courage. Lead me to live how You would have me live. Amen."

We have come a long way – wow! We are living these steps, repeating these steps, implementing the tools into our lives and continuously taking action to become who God created us to be. Up to this point, we've been on this journey with God, our confessor, and ourselves. What are your thoughts about reaching out to others? Making amends? Let's talk about that next.

Keeping it Personal

1. At the beginning of the chapter, we learned our actions produce 1 of 2 reactions. Which reaction have you been causing?

2. What does being intentional about your spiritual growth look like? What are some things that you could implement into your life to ensure your continued journey to overcome, refine, become?

3. Have you experienced consequential feelings of humiliation or embarrassment as a result of your actions? Are you willing to learn from those times and seek to identify what shortcomings in your life resulted in those consequences?

4. We've seen a lot of "less than desirable" things about ourselves. According to what you have read, how do you separate yourself from the "ickiness"?

5. Are you ready to trust God completely? Have you humbly let Him have the driver's seat of your life and acknowledged that His future is the only future for you?

CHAPTER 9

RESPONSIBILITY

STEP 8:

Made a list of all persons we had harmed, and became
willing to make amends to them all.

MY TOOL:

I need to make a list of those whom I have harmed; to become willing
to set the wrong right; to apologize. I must also make a list of those
whom I need to forgive and become willing to forgive them.

*"When you hold resentment toward another, you are bound to that
person or condition by an emotional link that is stronger than steel.
Forgiveness is the only way to dissolve that link and get free."*

—CATHERINE PONDER

Really? You want me to do what? Make amends to others? This may feel like the weight of the world on your shoulders. I know it did for me. I had instant anxiety – butterflies in my stomach just thinking of the people whose names would make it onto my list.

We've found the courage to dig deep. We've made a list already, our searching and fearless inventory. It's in black and white. Many things were revealed to us, and from those revelations we identified whom we have hurt, been dishonest with, disrespectful to, or harmed in any way. We've also started to identify whom we have not forgiven, whom we are angry with or holding resentment towards. And now, I need to be willing to set my wrongs right, regardless of how difficult it may seem? I have to forgive?

Fortunately, the answer is *yes*. I use the word "fortunately" because this is an opportunity. It's our opportunity to walk through the pain and experience freedom on the other side. If we do nothing with what we've uncovered, if we stop now and just review our inventory, the accounting of our life, and do nothing with it, we will stay bound to it; spiritually and emotionally stuck, sick. We want victory, do we not? We want change, right?

Choosing to not work this step would be choosing to hold onto the pain. Pain is mental or emotional suffering; it hurts and is not healthy. When we hold onto pain we are wounded, and through our wounds we will wound others. We cannot live a life completely pain-free; pain is inevitable. But suffering is optional. If we want change, then we need to be the change that we want to see. There is a crucial need to take more action. We are equipped with our tools in our toolbox; willingness, acceptance, faith, surrender, and courage. This is our next step and yes, we must take it.

We've come to a very important moment, almost a growing-up experience. In Chapter Two, where we picked up our first tool, Acceptance, I talked about pulling up our bootstraps. Now is the time we need to put on our big boy pants. When we are living in and stuck in the after-effects of our Nevers, we are hanging onto hurts, misery, and lies. This causes us to live in an illusion. We are unable to see our part, our role in the situation or experience. But now we're coming into the light, discovering truth, and our view of ourselves is coming into alignment with God's view of us. We can see that the ways in which we've treated others were not always the best, and the lack of forgiveness and resentments that we are harboring confine us and hold us captive. This is the blockage that separates us from being fully alive and from becoming who we were created to be. It keeps us from discovering our life purpose.

The step says, "Made a list of all the persons we had harmed." The best place to start to make our new list is to review our first list, the one you developed with courage in Chapter Five. With pen in hand, take out a fresh piece of paper. You will break this down four ways.

First, look at your written inventory, the first list. Write down the name of each person that causes you to feel icky, uneasy, or restless – some sort of emotional pain.

Second, peel back the layers identifying where you may have been wrong. Ask yourself these questions, "What did I do to set the ball in motion?" or "What did I do to keep the ball rolling?" Pay no attention to how others have hurt you or how you had been wronged. For the purposes of this list, we are only looking at our own side of the street.

Believe me, I know this can be extremely difficult to do. But we are taking responsibility for ourselves, and this is our pain, these are our hurts, and our path to walk. What others do is their business. Next to each name, write your answer to these questions:

* *Where have you been wrong?*

* *What could you have done differently?*

It's important to understand here that not every one of these people or experiences on your list will have an answer. Perhaps you were wounded by someone as an innocent child, or were taken advantage of in a vulnerable situation, or maybe you were a victim of a terrible act in which things were done to you. We cannot take responsibility for these things; none of that is ever right. But keep the name on the list, there is a reason it is there. Most likely the lingering after-effects are still there, and something is unresolved that needs to be dealt with.

Third, honestly write your current feelings towards the person, place, or situation. If you are stuck and having a hard time naming your feelings, print off a list of feeling words from my website, **keepingitpersonal.com/tools.**

This list might help you give your emotions a name.

Fourth, ask yourself – are you still angry, harboring ill feelings, unforgiveness, resentment? Write your answer – yes or no. (You can download a worksheet for this exercise on my website **keepingitpersonal.com/tools.**)

Something extremely powerful happens when we make our list. We are taking action, growing, and working through our struggles. The transferring of information from our heads onto something that we can visibly see starts the reconciliation process and begins bringing healing to our hearts. It gets us one step closer to freedom, one step closer to Promised Land living. Did you do it? Did you make the new list?

Assuming you did make the new list, I'm curious as to whether your own name was on it. Did you put yourself on the list? Are *you* someone with whom you need to make amends? How is your relationship with yourself? Do you love, accept, and approve of who you are and the things that you've done? Have you forgiven yourself for past mistakes, for wrong decisions? Are you resentful towards yourself, angry about whom you've become, and feeling regret? If your answer to any of these questions is *yes*, and you're not on the list, get your name on there! The most important relationship in the whole wide world is the relationship we have with ourselves. If we cannot love, accept, and forgive ourselves, we will remain stuck. If we cannot receive and accept grace for our lives, how can we offer forgiveness, love and grace towards others?

How about God – did He make the list? Are you angry with Him? Are you resentful about the cards that have been dealt to you? Do you hold Him responsible for the hurts, pains, and losses in your life? If so, He should be on the list as well, if He's not already.

When I arrived at this step and decided I was ready to take responsibility, I made my list in my Blackberry. Each of us has our own unique way of doing things, you need to do what works best for you, and that is what worked best for me. I felt that having my list on my phone and with me at all times was important. It was my reminder of taking action and continuing on this journey.

Next, the step says, "and became willing." This is a process: "we became." We do not need to march out and do this immediately; knock on doors, write letters, make phone calls, or send emails. We have not necessarily, all of a sudden, just instantly, arrived at a place where we can do this. So, take a deep breath and let's work through this together, putting one foot in front of the other.

Willingness. Here we are again with that word. It has become a staple that holds all the tools together. Imagine a tool box carrying all of our tools – this tool box would have the word "willingness" plastered all around it. It sounds a little silly, I know, but each step we take is taken with willingness; no one is making us do what we are doing. Each time we pick up a tool, we implement it with willingness; no one is taking this action for us. Our tools are contained in our willingness box.

The question now is, are you willing to make amends to them all? Not just one or two of them, but everyone on your list? (And if you're wondering about how or if you can make amends with someone who is no longer in your life, or of whom you have lost track, or who may not be living – you can. There is a way that we will talk about in the next chapter.) Don't answer this question until you understand what it really means to make amends.

To amend is to improve or correct something; it's making it better. When we make amends, we are not out to fix others, a past situation, or a relationship. We are taking responsibility for our part. We are willing to set a wrong "right" or "square-up." We have no idea what the result will be when we take action with our list. Our only concern when making amends should be to do what's right.

Think of this as recovery mode. This may seem selfish, but making amends is about you and for you. It's for your personal healing and growth. It's an act of returning to "normal" – it's the regaining of, or the possibility of, regaining something lost or taken away; a restoration or a return to health from sickness. Making amends will breathe new life into you, open doors to new opportunities, and is the start of new beginnings. It's freedom.

To sum up this step and to grasp the responsibility tool, we are simply apologizing and forgiving. I know, it's not simple to do, but the concept is elementary. By being the change you want to see – by taking this step – there will be healing in your own life, and don't be surprised to see healing in the life of another.

Keeping it Personal

1. If forgiveness is an opportunity to experience freedom on the other side, what does that freedom look like for you?

2. How long have you held on to the pain? What keeps you holding on?

3. How has your perspective changed since we have focused only on your "side of the street"?

4. Were you surprised if you and/or God made it onto your list? Why or why not?

5. Do you act as if someone is making choices for you? As if someone is making you act in certain ways?

CHAPTER 10

RESTORATION

STEP 9:
Made direct amends to such people wherever possible,
except when to do so would injure them or others.

MY TOOL:
Take action; start the restoration process. Be cautious, and considerate
not to injure others – pray and ask God for guidance. Ask Him to
prepare the hearts of those with whom you need to connect.

*"It is the highest form of self-respect to admit our errors
and mistakes and make amends for them. To make a
mistake is only an error in judgment, but to adhere to it
when it is discovered shows infirmity of character."*
— DALE E. TURNER

U p to this point, our journey through the steps, and the process of learning these tools, has been pretty private. We've worked extremely hard internally – on our heart, with ourselves and God – except for the work we did in Chapter Six, which was where we admitted the exact nature of our wrongs with another human being. Now, it's time we do some external work.

This is the 4th and final step which starts with the word "made." "Made" is past tense for "make" – which implies we've done this. When we make, we create and build. "Making" is a verb; it's taking action, accomplishing, forging forward, and producing. First, we made a decision to turn our will and our lives over to the care of God as we understood Him: surrender. Second, we made a searching and fearless moral inventory of ourselves: courage. Third, we made a list of all persons we had harmed, and became willing to make amends to them all: responsibility. And now, fourth, we made direct amends. Before these things can be made, we must first be willing to "make" – by implementing our tools.

I wanted to share this observation with you in order to drive home the point that this toolbox is all about taking action. We are taking these steps – applying them into our lives – living and using these tools. We need to be intentional every day to create, build, and become. Are you with me? If so, let's experience restoration and make direct amends.

With this tool, the rubber meets the road. We've pulled up our boot straps, we've got on our big boy pants, and we are rolling up our sleeves and going to work – we are dressed and ready to go. We are going to them with a helpful and forgiving spirit. We stand tall, understanding what we must do – apologize and forgive. We clearly understand why we must do it – for restoration, healing, growth, and freedom.

We must implement this tool with the right attitudes – courage, caution, and good judgment – and in the right way, with a careful sense of appropriate timing. We are willing and equipped with eight tools thus far. We need to trust God to guide us and we need to pray, asking Him to show us where to start and how to make these direct amends. We may not see the solution until we take the first step of faith. Remember, you are not responsible for the outcome, only for being obedient and doing the right thing. This is faith, trusting that God is in total control. Gentleness is what we seek, for ourselves and with others.

These direct amends do not have to be made all at once, but we must wrap our arms around those two scary words; "action now." There are three potential stumbling blocks that could trip you up and keep you from taking action now.

First is pride, the poisonous kind that doesn't allow us to see our own fault, to sincerely seek to understand where we could be wrong, or to see the importance of forgiveness. This pride puts blinders on our eyes and fogs our glasses. It's selfish and narrow-minded, the opposite of humility. Couple this with our ego, and our spiritual growth will come to a screeching halt. Pride prevents us from moving forward, from taking responsibility, and from restoration.

Second, fear. What will others think of me? What happens if it doesn't go well? What if they reject me? When we are too concerned about what others will think about us if we "admit" where we were wrong or open ourselves up to offer forgiveness, blockage will remain between us and our Source, God. If we are consumed with thoughts like *this is weak*, we will be stuck. Fear is assumptive; it is false evidence appearing real. We need to step out in faith, following God's lead, and move through the fear.

Third, minimizing. Fear to face our pain head-on can create a temptation to minimize. Dismissing our feelings of anger, resentment, and lack of forgiveness towards someone who has wounded us, is an excuse. Having the attitude that what we've done really wasn't that big of a deal, or that the role we played didn't have much impact on the situation, is also an excuse. The people on our list made it on our list for specific reasons. Minimizing will set us back, because it allows us to overlook the work that needs to be done. We need to overcome the lingering after-effects of experiencing our Nevers. Whether big or small, our feelings are real and alive.

If one or all of these things are stumbling blocks for you, dig into your willingness tool box and put some oil on your tools; acceptance, faith, surrender, courage, admission, humility, transformation. Identify what's missing or what area needs work so that you can take action – now.

Making amends is where we win. When we live out this step with others in our lives, ourselves, and God, we are showing compassion. This demonstration extends consideration and kindness. It brings us together and breaks down barriers. We are overcoming evil with good, human to human, as equals. Our changed behavior and new attitudes are the evidence or expression of what has happened and what continues to happen within us. Growing into these steps and walking them out daily is our display of proof. We do not need to wear our spirituality "on our sleeves." We do not need to plaster a neon sign on our foreheads announcing what we are doing, because our actions will speak much louder than our words. Remember who your audience is; God. Remember that your goal is to clean up your side of the street. Remember, you are not responsible for the outcome, only to do what is right.

How do we take action? How do we make amends and forgive? Let's look at these separately.

To make amends is essentially to apologize. I like the word "apologize" better, because it's clearer to me, so I'm choosing to go with that word as we talk about this process. As we discussed in the last chapter, to make amends is to make better. We do this by expressing remorse through offering a formal apology. To do this, we must be clear about what we are apologizing for.

When I got to this step, I took action before I truly understood what this meant. I learned a big lesson the hard way that I would like to share with you. There is not a formal "right" way to apologize – each expression should be authentic and come from our hearts. But I can tell you that there are more effective ways than others to communicate. Let me share with you what I mean.

God clearly revealed to me a person to whom I needed to make amends. It was weighing heavily on my heart. I took action by sending an email. It wasn't very long; here is the body of what I wrote, "…I want to apologize to you for anything that I might have done to harm you, or said to hurt your feelings, or if I have caused pain to you in any way…" This was a very sincere attempt and it came from my heart. I had the desire to restore our relationship. But, there was a problem with this attempt – I used the words "might" and "if." I wasn't taking specific responsibility. We dialogued back and forth via email and essentially got nowhere. I felt I was worse off after this attempt to apologize than I was before I had started.

Because there was no resolution, this person still weighed heavily on my heart. I had the sincere desire to set the wrong right. I just needed to communicate it more effectively. So, approximately six weeks later, I felt God tugging on my heart again. By this time, He had revealed to me specific areas in which I had been wrong. I was able to take responsibility for my role and identify how I set the ball in motion.

With this new knowledge, I composed a new email. This is an excerpt of what I wrote, "…I was wrong! When I got real honest with myself, I realized that I was selfish and my motives were self-seeking. I wanted you to move back so that I could spend more time with you. The very thing that I wanted, I never got. Yes, my intentions, I thought, were being helpful at the time. But when I seriously look at the situation from the very beginning and get really honest with myself on how I set the ball rolling – I was wrong! I have the sincere desire to set this wrong right. Please let me know what I can do…" This approach prompted my friend to call me. Through voicemails and a couple of brief conversations, she accepted my apology, and we offered forgiveness to one another. That is making amends. That is restoration, healing, freedom. Our relationship is nothing like it had been in the past. We do not talk frequently or spend time together, but it's okay. I trusted God with the outcome and I trust Him with what the future holds for our relationship.

Do you see the difference in the two approaches? One is taking responsibility and is specific; the other is not. When we make direct amends, we need to take responsibility. We need to be clear about what we are apologizing for. I am so grateful that I learned this lesson, and I have been amazed at how gracious others have been with me as I seek to set my wrongs right.

Next, I want to address our expectations. The bottom line is, we can't have any expectations for the outcome or the recipient. If we implement this tool with expectation, we will most likely be disappointed. Our only expectation should be placed on God – that He is in control of the results and that His will be done, not our will. We are walking in faith. We are obedient to what He is calling us to do.

Honesty is crucial in our approach. We are seeking restoration which can be healing not only to you, but also to the other person involved. Our primary focus when we apologize is to take responsibility and clean up our side of the street.

It is important that we also share ways that we have been hurt. This is a very delicate topic, because we are approaching them. We are going out to them; they have not asked to hear our hurts and feelings. However, as I've grown in this step and as I continue to implement this tool, I've realized the importance of sharing this in honesty.

We place no blame. We do not accuse the other person of wrong-doing or tell them what they should've done differently. When the time is right, after we've had the opportunity to do what we need to do, we simply say, "I am hurt" or "I was hurt." We constructively share our feelings. When we are transparent in our approach, it gives others permission to be transparent. Again, managing our expectations when we share is crucial. We are not responsible for the outcome. We may never hear "I'm sorry." We many never get answers to our many questions. What they do with this knowledge of how you've been hurt is their responsibility. Their response is between them and God.

In the last chapter, we decided that we are willing to make amends to them all. There may be people on your list that you've lost track of or who are no longer living. The best approach to take in doing this work is to write letters that will never be sent. Pour out your heart on paper. Admit where you had been wrong, share your feelings, ask for forgiveness if that is necessary, say good-bye if it is appropriate.

That's what I did. I've written several letters that I knew I would never send, and I continue to do it. This method isn't new. Some call it letter-writing therapy. It has been helpful for me at times to read the letters out loud to others who I could trust. I pretend that I'm reading them to the person to whom they were written, and when I'm finished we discuss the situation. Do what works best for you – again, seeking God for guidance.

The letter-writing method works extremely well in matters between yourself and God. If your name and God's are on your list that you created, write the letters, hash it out with yourself, and be brutally honest with your feelings towards God. Nothing you feel or say to Him will make Him love you more, and nothing you feel or say will make Him love you less. He loves you with an unconditional love, and is waiting for you to accept and receive His forgiveness and grace. The most important relationship you can work on restoring is that with yourself. When you love and forgive yourself, it opens the door for you to receive love and forgiveness from God and others. As I was driving home yesterday praying about this chapter, God impressed upon my heart these thoughts, "What about those whom we do not know that we've hurt? Or those to whom we are not aware that we need to make an apology?"

We cannot set something right if we are not aware there is something wrong. We need not worry about the unknowns; at the proper time, we will become aware. Our attitude at all times must be willingness and the desire to respond positively.

If or when we are presented with knowledge that something that we've done or said has wounded someone, we have the opportunity to make amends at that moment. Up to this point, I have not had anyone come to me directly and share that I've harmed them. I have, however, been proactive and asked specific people this question, "Have I done something that has hurt you? Or have I caused you pain in any way?" A couple of people responded that I had hurt them. They were open to sharing with me their hurts and I was able to own my part. There are a few people who appreciated me asking and responded, "Nothing I would like to talk about now." But they know that at any time, I am willing to listen and answer questions about any event that has happened in the past. You see, we are not always aware how we impact the lives of others, but if we are approachable and honest, then we do not need to worry or fret about bumping into anyone in the aisle of a grocery store.

Each day, I choose to do my best. I am intentional about living these steps and work at implementing them into my life daily. But I can only act upon what I know. My desire is to remain approachable and open. I want to embrace others in love, be the fellow believer that someone can come to, as it says in Matthew 18:15 (The Message) "If a fellow believer hurts you, go and tell him—work it out between the two of you. If he listens, you've made a friend."

Making amends can go two ways. As you put yourself out there, be open to being approached. There is nothing more freeing than restoration in relationships with everyone.

Last but not least, I need to stress the importance of the last phrase of this step, "except when to do so would injure them or others." Do not be so zealous to wipe your slate clean that you harm others in the process. We go in courage, yes, but with caution, and good judgment. Seek guidance through prayer for the proper timing and the right words to say. If you are questioning any act of making amends even slightly, consider first seeking guidance from the person you worked with in Step Five, before taking action. Do not confuse making amends with confession to ourselves, God, and another human being (our confessor, not the person with whom we have the issue). Role play. Consider all angles. Go in love.

I know that the word "forgive" is not used in this step. Actually, it is not used in any of the steps. But forgiveness is part of the amends process; it happens subtly when we reach out and take responsibility with others for our actions and apologize. When we can admit where we've been wrong, we are starting the forgiveness process with others, and we are also starting the forgiveness process with ourselves. Like I said, it's subtle, but it's shining light into a dark area. We begin to feel better about who we are because we are doing the right thing.

Forgiveness is letting go of resentment against, or the desire to punish, someone. When we forgive, we stop blaming and grant pardon; we give up anger. You may pose the argument that certain others are not worthy of forgiveness – that they are undeserving. My answer to that argument is this; are you yourself not in need of forgiveness for some transgression? How can we expect to be forgiven, but be unwilling to forgive others? We are all worthy of forgiveness. Do not let your deep wounds from others prevent you from breaking from anger, resentment, or an unforgiving attitude. The reality is that when we forgive, we are not sending the message that what happened is right or okay. Carol Luebering communicates boldly why we need to forgive, "Let's get one thing straight: forgiving is not something you do for someone else. You need to forgive so that you can move forward with life. An unforgiven injury binds you to a time and place someone else has chosen; it holds you trapped in a past moment and in old feelings."

Here we are; we must forgive in order to break the bond that ties us negatively to others, and also so that we can be forgiven. Forgiveness comes from our hearts. This is between us and God – we do not need to let others know that we have forgiven them, unless the opportunity presents itself and it is appropriate.

There are many books and articles written about forgiveness, giving us step-by-step instructions. For some, forgiveness can be as simple as just deciding not to be mad anymore. For others, it's not so easy to let go. I've found that the method of forgiveness that works best for me is the one shared by Emmet Fox in his explanation of the Lord's Prayer. Let's not reinvent the wheel – this has been used by many people since the 1930's. It's direct and precise:

"The method of forgiving is this: Get by yourself and become quiet. Repeat any prayer or treatment that appeals to you, or read a chapter of the Bible. Then quietly say, 'I fully and freely forgive X (mentioning the name of the offender); I lose him and let him go. I completely forgive the whole business in question. As far as I'm concerned, it is finished forever. I cast the burden or resentment upon the Christ within me. He is free now, and I am free too. I wish him well in every phase of his life. The incident is finished. The Christ Truth has set us both free. I thank God.' Then get up and go about your business. On no account repeat this act of forgiveness, because you have done it once and for all, and to do it a second time would be tacitly to repudiate your own work. Afterward, whenever the memory of the offender or the offense happens to come into your mind, bless the delinquent briefly and dismiss the thought. Do this, however many times the thought may come back. After a few days it will return less and less often, until you forget it altogether. Then perhaps after an interval, shorter or longer, the old trouble may come back to memory once more, but you will find that now all bitterness and resentment have disappeared, and you are both free with the perfect freedom of the children

of God. Your forgiveness is complete. You will experience a wonderful joy in the realization of the demonstration.[2]

That's it. I'm here to tell you, this method works. When you are ready, go through your list and sincerely pray this prayer for each person. When thoughts come back, which they will – they have and still do for me, from time to time – whisper a prayer of blessing upon that person and dismiss the thought. Fix your mind on things above. Focus on your blessings and the many positive things in your life.

---

2 Emmet Fox, *The Sermon on the Mount: The Key to Success in Life*, (New York: Harper Collins, 1989), "A Forgiveness Technique."

Keeping it Personal

1. Have your "makes" all become "mades" so far? Have you taken action, and followed the previous steps?

2. When was the last time you said, "I'm sorry" and really meant it?

3. Pride, selfishness, self-centeredness – how will you begin to peel back these layers?

4. What is your biggest fear about making amends?

5. What feelings have you attempted to dismiss as insignificant, unimportant?

CHAPTER 11

CLARITY

STEP 10:

Continued to take personal inventory and when
we were wrong promptly admitted it.

MY TOOL:

Look in the mirror and evaluate your life daily. Look for anything that
has built up or created blockage between you and God. Take action to
clean your slate by implementing the tools. Embrace the positives.

*"Test yourselves to make sure you are solid in the faith. Don't drift
along taking everything for granted. Give yourselves regular checkups.
You need firsthand evidence, not mere hearsay, that Jesus Christ is
in you. Test it out. If you fail the test, do something about it."*

—2 CORINTHIANS 13:5 {MESSAGE}

We are choosing to grow. Isn't it exciting? No one can stop us! With each step we take, with each tool we learn and implement into our life, we are polishing our hearts. Through rubbing and friction, by doing hard things, we are becoming; being refined to sparkle, to shine, to brighten our world. The more we polish, the more we are aware of ourselves, our needs, our purpose, His will, and His plan for us.

With courage, in Chapter Five, we made a searching and fearless moral inventory of ourselves. Now, along those same lines, we continue to take personal inventory. Another action word, "continue." We go on, keep on. We endure. We last. This journey to grow will never end. There is no ceiling to our becoming who we were created to be – are you willing to continue? If so, let's explore how we can intentionally look in the mirror daily to evaluate and take personal inventory.

We can compare this journey to a fitness plan – but instead of getting physically fit and building up muscle strength and endurance, we are working to get spiritually, emotionally, and faithfully fit. It's easy to stop and rest; that's why each day we must be deliberate about what we do. We must persevere and make forward progress. This step, clarity, and the remaining two steps, awareness and light, are the steps that will help you sustain your growth. If you continue to choose to grow, they will be the tools that you need to keep up and maintain your "fitness."

By now you are well aware that this book, these steps, and each tool is about you. The focus is not on others – it is on you. Each of us is forever changing and forever growing. What we've done up to this point is amazing work, is admirable and praiseworthy – but this is just the beginning. We have scratched the surface. As we live and grow, we will discover truth and answers from ourselves, by taking inventory. A personal reflection each day will disclose that which is negative so that we will work appropriately, to overcome what we discover, then we can grow in our positive living. We will also pay attention to our strengths, acknowledge what we are grateful for, and count our blessings. We will clean our house daily with the ultimate goal of our inside matching our outside – wholeness.

What does this look like, continuing to take personal inventory? At first, I would suggest scheduling it into your day, each night for example, to get in the habit of doing it. That's what I did. Each night before I fell asleep I whispered my simple little prayer, "Father, open my eyes to see, open my ears to hear, open my heart to know. Amen." Then I started reflecting on my day. Keeping a journal is helpful and can be a great tool in tracking your progress. If you're not the journaling type, I've created a checklist that you can print off my website: **keepingitpersonal.com/tools**. This is a personal program, so do what works best for you. As you develop this habit and become more aware, you will find yourself doing small spot-check invento-ries throughout the day. This has become true for me. When I feel uneasy inside or sense a "storm" rising up inside of me, when I feel my face becoming flushed, or sense the stirrings of anxiety – I'm instantly prompted to tap into my tool box. It took me some time to arrive at this place of maintenance, but with practice you, too, will get there.

What are your triggers? It's important to get clear and identify what the symptoms are of the things that cause our "storms." You know what I'm talking about, right? The things that make your blood boil or that push your buttons? Use whatever terminology you like. The more clarity you have, the quicker you will be able to respond to each "storm" and work through it positively.

We can divide our daily inventory into four categories for the purpose of looking at our attitudes and character. The most important relationship we have is with ourselves, so let's start there.

YOU: How did you treat you today? How did you talk to yourself today? Were you hard on yourself – telling yourself lies, like *I'm stupid, I'm not good enough, I'm a failure?* Or did you love and affirm yourself? Did you tell yourself, *it's okay to make mistakes; I've got everything it takes to be successful and prosperous; I am loveable and everyone is blessed to know me?* Are you feeling shame or guilt over an experience that happened? Did you have an unfavorable interaction that left you feeling embarrassed or regretful? Did your mind take you to a place where you allowed your past to haunt you? How are you feeling about yourself today? Are you angry, resentful, or restless? Are you sulking in negativity, having a pity party? Are you complaining and being critical? OR, are you grateful for what you have, thinking about your blessings and the positive assets in your life?

OTHERS: How did you treat others today? Were you loving, patient, kind, tolerant, and understanding? Or were you irritable and frustrated? Were you helpful and looking for ways to encourage and lift up those around you? Or were you critical and finding fault? Were you honest about others and with others? Was your tongue tame today; did your words destroy, or lift up? Did you live by the Golden Rule and treat others the way that you would want to be treated?

GOD: This is a heart condition, the supernatural connection you feel. Did your actions, thoughts, and motives put a smile on God's face? What blockage stands between you and God? Is there anything that is preventing you from receiving His love and grace? Are you harboring feelings of anger, fear, jealousy, envy, self-pity, resentment, or selfishness? Are you feeling and experiencing the fruits of the Spirit: love, joy, peace, patience, kindness, goodness, faithfulness, gentleness and self-control?

LIFE: What did I contribute to the day? What did I take from the day? What were the highs and lows? What were the ups and downs? What am I grateful for? What blessed me today? Did I sow positivity or negativity into the stream of life today?

We are renewing our mind when we take this time to reflect. My husband calls it recharging. It's a restoring or replenishing, taking time out to evaluate our progress. This is the ongoing process that we need for improvement. We are not looking for perfection; rather, for development, improvement, and betterment.

If we stumble or mess up, if we revert back to old behaviors, we don't despair or fret: we simply pick ourselves up and dust ourselves off. The last part of this step says, "When we were wrong, promptly admitted it." What does this look like in our daily living? We can use our tools to make amends, forgive, or resolve anything that came into the light from our inventory; take the time necessary for reflection. We live in the now, taking one day at a time. We seek to enjoy the present, the gift of life we have each day.

Clarity comes when we see what's at our core, the underlying issues that prompt us to respond to others or life situations negatively. To get to this level of clarity, we must peel back the layers of our feelings by continuing to ask ourselves the crucial question, *why?* Let me share with you an example of what this could look like, in this very familiar situation.

Becky was resentful because her boyfriend Sam had told her that they were going to have a quiet weekend together. Then, unexpectedly, Sam's friend showed up from out of town. Sam offered to let his friend stay with them at their home for the weekend. This was not earth-shattering, but Becky was extremely annoyed and resentful towards Sam's friend for imposing on them, and angry with Sam for extending the offer without talking with her about it. Becky had a storm raging inside of her. She was short in her interactions with Sam, rude to Sam's friend, and moped around the house all weekend with a chip on her shoulder. Becky's expectations of quality time with Sam went out the window. She was not happy.

Let's peel back the layers, starting with why Becky was resentful. She had wanted a quiet weekend and quality alone time with Sam. When Sam offered accommodations to his friend for the weekend, Becky felt angry and mad. She felt that her feelings didn't matter, that she didn't have a voice, and that she was unimportant.

Let's continue to peel them back: Why was she angry and mad? Becky was feeling sad and lonely. She had feelings of not being good enough. She felt Sam chose his friend over her. Becky had hurt feelings; she wanted to feel special and important. Sam's actions left her feeling unloved.

Instead of responding negatively as Becky chose to do, it would've been better for her to choose to be honest and communicate her feelings to Sam. How does Becky work through her anger and resentment towards that situation? She must make amends with Sam.

She must say honestly, "I understand you want to help your friend and I admire you for that quality. I was wrong to be short with you all weekend and rude to your friend. But I need to share that I'm really hurt that you made that decision without talking to me first. I was looking forward to spending quality time together this weekend. When you made that decision without talking with me, I felt unloved, unimportant, and sad. I was looking forward to it being just you and me. I miss you."

Remember, when we make amends and share our feelings, we do it without expectations. We are tapping into our toolbox, and we are implementing acceptance and courage. We are taking responsibility. After we communicate our feelings, we forgive and bless – and we move on.

Make this a daily practice. Actively make amends, continuously cleaning up your side of the street. Forgive others, allowing you to break free. Again, I want to mention the importance of recognizing our triggers. We have to acknowledge those feelings that our triggers bring to the surface, and how they prompt us to respond.

Another common example to be aware of is selfishness. This one sneaks in quietly. People think, "I'm not selfish, because I do everything for everybody else. I give of my time. I give this, I give that – I'm not selfish. Nobody ever does anything for me. I'm the one that gives and gives." The reality is that some of those "giving" people are the most selfish people. Why? Because of their motives and the reasons behind their giving. If you get angry, upset, or mad when things don't work out the way you wanted them to, after you've given or poured out yourself – you might be operating out of selfishness. It's potentially a control issue that you're not being honest with yourself about; a control issue that you're trying to turn into a virtue.

Honesty goes hand-in-hand with clarity. Say *yes* when you mean *yes* and *no* when you mean *no*. You cannot have clarity unless you're being completely honest with yourself. I'm not talking about the lying-versus-the-truth kind of honesty; I'm talking about being honest with our feelings. As you grow in this step and practice peeling back the layers, you will recognize more and more what you're feeling when you're feeling it. Many of us have spent most of our lives putting everyone else's needs in front of ours, thinking that we're selfless, when in fact we're being selfish because we're doing it for the wrong reasons.

How can you judge if what you're feeling is justifiable, and not just a symptom of something else, or an excuse? We all have God-given good and bad feelings. When we are angry or feeling the "bad" feelings, that should prompt us to dig deeper and find out what sparked these feelings. Obviously something stole our joy or faith in the outcome. Anger is a valid feeling. Feeling sadness is okay. Again, though, peel back the layers and figure out where the sadness really comes from. As in the example above, Becky wasn't sad because Sam had a friend over, but because it made her feel unloved. "I'm sad because I feel like I'm in second place. I'm sad because I thought that you would respect my feelings and ask me what to do instead of just making that decision on your own." We can still feel sadness, and not have a storm as long as we recognize it and communicate our feelings honestly.

We need to keep this tool ever-present in our mind, because this step, clarity, takes work. Sometimes, I have to admit, I just want to be ticked off and blame everyone else. Other times, I'm tired of doing the right thing – always looking in the mirror to determine where I've been wrong. *What about everyone else, look at what they're doing – they are not perfect!* Sometimes my attitude is negative and ugly. But you know what? I don't really like it there. It's dark and cold. When I'm angry and want to put the blame on others, I don't experience the good stuff, the fruit; love, joy, peace, and freedom.

To effectively apply this tool in your life every day, you need to go through your personal checklist, and ask yourself honestly – *is there anyone that I've harmed today? Was I dishonest with myself or my feelings today? Is there a situation or a place or a thing that is causing me any pain or bad feelings?* Now is the time to identify it. If you are struggling personally in your relationship with yourself, comfort yourself, journal about it, "hold your own hand" in a sense. Take care of you, because nobody else is going to.

How can you see yourself more clearly? By continuing to look at your pain, by refusing to put your blinders back on. By acknowledging when you feel it and not instantly going into the blame game – which is so easy to do. *I'm feeling this way, a storm, that person must be wrong. No, I'm feeling this way, what did I do? Where's my heart? Where's my faith? Where's my willingness? Where's my acceptance? Are my expectations taking control? Are my rights in the way?* By asking ourselves those questions, and going back to acceptance, our first tool, we begin to progress through the seemingly endless maze of feelings that clog our hearts, our minds and our lives. As we continue to do this, and to admit our wrongs, our lives become clearer and our paths straighter. Our relationship with ourselves, with others, and with God becomes richer and more meaningful. Instead of a constant cycle of confusion, we experience an ever-improving cycle of honesty, truth and forgiveness.

Keeping it Personal

1. Are you willing to commit each day to allow God (your "Personal Trainer") to show you areas that need work?

2. Is your heart thankful?

3. How did it make you feel to evaluate your treatment of you?

4. Do you think your treatment of you affected your treatment of others?

5. How are you choosing to enjoy your present today?

CHAPTER 12

AWARENESS

STEP 11:

Sought through prayer and meditation to improve our conscious contact with God, as we understood Him, praying only for knowledge of His will for us and the power to carry that out.

MY TOOL:

Pray AND listen. We must do both in our own way. Connect with God, asking and praying for knowledge of His will for our lives, and the power, strength, and wisdom to carry it out. Listen; meditate to receive the answers, which come through thoughts, people, situations, and experiences.

"Don't ask what the world needs. Ask what makes you come alive, and go do it. Because what the world needs is people who have come alive."

— HOWARD THURMAN

Imagine for a moment that your soul is a cup whose contents you pour out through your day, a cup which periodically needs to be refilled. Just as our bodies need proper food and nourishment to function effectively, to thrive and grow – so do our souls. I call this my soul food; prayer and meditation. It has become such an essential part of my life that I cannot go without it and feel good. Notice I said, I cannot go without it and feel "good." I can go without it, sure, but when I do, I feel that something is missing. I feel empty. I feel I am running on fumes emotionally with everyone in my life and I have nothing to give. I get frustrated and irritable. I have a short fuse. When I don't take the time to implement this tool in my life, it also affects me physically. I tire easily and become unorganized because I am flying by the seat of my pants.

Life is very full. Most of us wear many hats; we work, we parent, we are spouses, significant others, employees, siblings, and friends. We volunteer, and we are involved with church. With each hat we wear, we pour out of ourselves a little or a lot of who we are. We give of ourselves.

Let's go back to imagining that you are a cup. If you continue to pour out your cup into each area of your life, but neglect getting your cup filled or replenished, you will be empty – you will become dry. We are responsible for taking care of ourselves and understanding our needs. You cannot be filled up or absorb your soul food without feeding yourself, another action we must take intentionally.

To sustain our journey of overcoming the Nevers, awareness is crucial. It keeps us alive, focused, and moving forward. We've learned how to use the tools we need to garden our lives. Now, let's personalize this step, by breaking it down so that we can gather seeds of truth.

This step says "sought," which is past tense for seek. We must seek and search for the truth by taking action to find or discover it, by exploring or questioning. The Bible says in Matthew 7:7, "Keep on asking, and you will receive what you ask for. Keep on seeking, and you will find. Keep on knocking, and the door will be opened to you." Keep on keeping on. Walk seeking awareness. We are on a quest, forever.

How do we seek? Through prayer and meditation. Move from one to another; prayer and meditation. Not just through prayer, not just through meditation – through both. You see, prayer is when you talk to God and meditation is when you listen to God.

For any relationship to develop and become valuable, two people need to get to know each other. I've experienced several one-sided relationships in my life – have you? They are not very fruitful. I don't enjoy trying to connect with someone who's only interested in talking about himself or herself and doesn't let me get a word in edgewise. On the flip side, I don't enjoy trying to connect with someone who is unwilling to open up and share with me anything about his or her life. Either of these mismatches makes for a one-sided relationship, and over time, usually not much time, they will fizzle. They are not mutual, they are shallow, and unless changes are made there is no substance to build upon.

The same is true in our relationship with God. In order for our connection to grow and become meaningful, we must talk and listen.

What does this look like? Each relationship we have here on earth is unique and special – and so is our personal relationship with God. There is no right way or wrong way to pray and meditate, but we must do it. We need to develop and "improve our conscious contact with God as we understood Him," as the step states. We have no user manuals to give us step-by-step instructions. Jesus teaches us how to pray through The Lord's Prayer, an outline providing us with tremendous value, which I embrace. But we were created to uniquely love, serve, and worship our Creator, and He's equipped us to do this with Him.

I will share with you what this looks like for me, how my personal relationship grows with God, but know that He wants to capture your heart and have you love Him in your own special way.

We talk with God by praying; this is our connection to Him. Prayer is a sincere petition to God, a spiritual communion with God; a request, thanksgiving, adoration, or confession. I shared with you in Chapter Three about my faith and how I whisper "popcorn" prayers frequently throughout the day. I have an ongoing conversation with God from the time I wake up to the time I go to bed. Sometimes I fall asleep at night praying and reflecting about my day, and I wake up in the morning continuing along the same lines. I love it.

Each day looks different. Some days I connect with Him more than others, it just depends. I am not rigid. I give myself grace. I have no set rules or guidelines other than what it says in this step, "praying only for knowledge of God's will for us and the power to carry that out." What that means to me is that I must continually pray that His will be done, not my will; surrendering every moment of every day. It doesn't mean that I cannot be real and authentic with God in sharing with Him my fears, hurts, raw emotions, dreams, and desires – I can. But I rest and trust in His promise that His plans for me are for good.

I pray for wisdom, guidance, and strength. I consistently ask Him to lead me and show me my next step. I pray my simple prayer, "Open my eyes to see, open my ears to hear, open my heart to know." I can see a smile on His face in my mind when I pray this way. I believe He enjoys hearing my heart, what I'm grateful for, and my desire to have Him lead me. I also believe He is honored when I need Him and rely solely upon Him to meet my every need.

There are times when I feel distant and as if my prayers are hitting the ceiling. I have resolved to continue to seek Him during these times. I know I am not alone – even when I feel at times that I am. As I persevere through these feelings, He shows up. He is faithful, He meets me where I am.

Another way I pray is by singing. I love music – inspirational uplifting Christian music often gives me the words I need to say, so I make these songs my prayers. I praise and worship Him in my car, around my house as I work, while I'm running with my iPod, and at church services.

Additionally, I seek out others to pray with me and for me. "When two of you get together on anything at all on earth and make a prayer of it, my Father in heaven goes into action. And when two or three of you are together because of me, you can be sure that I'll be there." (Matthew 18:20, The Message.) I regularly meet with a friend who prays for healing, deliverance, and blessings in my life. God continues to fill me up from the inside and gives me strength.

Prayer is powerful. Communicate and connect with God through prayer in a way that works best for you. If this is new to you, simply start by asking Him to show you how to pray. Remember our staple that holds all these tools together is our willingness toolbox.

Remain willing to seek God through prayer; simply being "willing to be willing" is all He needs. He will draw near to you as you draw near to Him. Plant this prayer seed, continue to water it daily, and it will grow. Soon you will develop your personal love language with God, through your prayers.

We have two ears for a reason; it's important to listen. Meditation is listening. Is it more important to meditate than to pray? No. Both are equally important. But listening can be more difficult to do; it takes patience and practice to learn. In our instant society, we want everything when we want it, now. I've often thought it would be fabulous if God could communicate with me via text message or email so I could clearly hear Him and know exactly what His answers are for me, how He's leading me, and what His plans are for me. But, of course that is unrealistic, so the alternative is meditation; snail mail.

What is meditation? It's to engage in thought or contemplation; to reflect. It's to study, to think, to dream, and to plan. This too is unique and looks different for everyone. When I made the decision to be intentional about meditation, to seek answers, truth, and direction, I didn't know what it meant. I just expected that God would speak to me and show me, somehow. When I first prayed this prayer, "Open my eyes to see, open my ears to hear, open my heart to know," I had no clue what I was looking to see, or needing to hear or know. But He did, and He started to reveal Himself and Truth to me. When I was willing, He was able.

He impressed a desire to read His word heavily on my heart. So, my primary source of seeking God in meditation is through the Bible. Each morning, most days, I dig into the Word expecting Him to speak to me. I didn't know where to start in reading the Bible. I had tried to just sit down and start reading it in the past, but that didn't work. I needed structure and a plan to stick to. So, I went to the bookstore and purchased *The Message//REMIX Solo: An Uncommon Devotional*.³ It's a daily devotional that takes you through each book of the Bible from Genesis to Revelations, highlighting select verses and providing a unique, contemplative study for reflection, encouragement, and life application.

I coupled this with my *Life Application Study Bible*⁴ each morning. God began transforming my life in just a few short weeks. I started to see Him everywhere. He spoke to me through people: friends, family, and random strangers. I received answers to some questions through lyrics of songs, books, and sermons. He speaks to me through stillness and in quiet moments of reflection. He gives me insights and intuitive thoughts about situations in my life. He gives me words to speak when I have nothing to say.

I learn and gain knowledge through my experiences, though my pain, through my tears. As I continue to seek Him, I feel Him with me, guiding me, leading me. We are in relationship – I enjoy my time with Him. I want to meditate and enjoy the many nuggets I receive from Him.

As I seek Him through prayer, He reveals to me what I need to know through meditation. I am not always thrilled with His answers, nor do I always understand His timing, but again, I rest and trust in His promise that His plans for me are for good.

Our relationship is two-sided and healthy when I take time to do my part. When life gets busy and full, and I put Him on the back burner, I feel disconnected and overwhelmed. When seeking

---

3 Eugene H. Peterson, Jan Johnson, J.R. Briggs and Katie Peckham, *The Message//REMIX Solo: An Uncommon Devotional* (Colorado, NavPress).

4 For more information on New Life Application Bible Studies, visit www.newlivingtranslation.com/05discoverthenlt/lasb.asp.

Him and His guidance is not a priority, I find myself trying to figure out everything on my own – looking to other people and myself for the answers. Consequently, this leads to selfish, non-surrendered living, seeking my will, not His. My life gets messy when this piece is missing and it's my reminder to meditate.

Ask God to show you how to meditate. He will, because He wants to speak to you. He wants to reveal to you His plan, His will, and His purpose for you. His desire is to walk with you, to be in relationship with you – to lead you and guide you. He will show up and do his part. Will you do yours? Improve your conscious contact with God through meditation.

This is my favorite step, my favorite tool. One of the most exciting parts of my day is waking up in the morning to pray and meditate. I get my soul food, God fills my cup and I start my day on a solid foundation. Having knowledge, living informed and alert, is exciting. When you are aware and gain understanding, you start to connect dots and put pieces of this life puzzle together. There are not so many unanswered questions or fears, because God is meeting your needs. Life is full of optimism and goodness. God is my best friend; He's my loving, caring, sweet, compassionate Father. He's my big huggable teddy bear.

Keeping it Personal

1. How do you feel when you go without your soul food? What takes place in your life when you are spiritually empty?

2. What "hats" do you wear?

3. Is your relationship with God a two-way relationship? Are you listening?

4. Are you ready to submit your will to His? To trade in your plans for His future?

5. Go back and look at your "hats" – are they all meant to be worn by you? Does God want you to maybe relinquish one/some of them so He can empower you to wear the remaining hats to the best of your ability?

CHAPTER 13

LIGHT

STEP 12:

Having had a spiritual awakening as a result of these steps, we tried to carry this message to {others} alcoholics, and to practice these principles in all of our affairs.

MY TOOL:

God has changed me and continues to change me. I am not perfect, but each day I make progress implementing these tools in all areas of my life. I am a miracle; I have a story to tell. Whenever possible I will share my experience, strength, and hope to impact the lives of others.

"There are two ways of spreading light: to be the candle or the mirror that reflects it."

— EDITH WHARTON

This is it, our last step, and our final tool to discover and learn about; as the saying goes, it's "last but not least." Not least at all, because this step brings a bright, promising beginning as we use these tools together to be a light.

As with clarity and awareness, this tool is instrumental to sustain your spiritual growth. The common theme of taking action continues through with this step. This is our work, work we do not only for us, but also for God and for others.

The Bible says, "Just as the body is dead without breath, so also faith is dead without good works." James 2:26 (NLT) But our works do not define us or determine our value. Our works also do not earn us favor, just as without faith it is impossible to please God.

However, "having had a spiritual awakening as a result of these steps" – work will be our manifestation: it will happen as a result of living these principles. James 2:14-17 (The Message) paints a picture of this faith in action, "Dear friends, do you think you'll get anywhere in this if you learn all the right words but never do anything? Does merely talking about faith indicate that a person really has it? For instance, you come upon an old friend dressed in rags and half-starved and say, "Good morning, friend! Be clothed in Christ! Be filled with the Holy Spirit!" and walk off without providing so much as a coat or a cup of soup—where does that get you? Isn't it obvious that God-talk without God-acts is outrageous nonsense?"

I agree that it is nonsense, and I also believe it will be impossible if we stay actively connected to the vine, God. If we are the branches, connected to the vine daily – getting our cup full of His truth, love, and goodness – we will pour out our message.

What does it mean to have a spiritual awakening? If you ask a hundred people this question, you might receive a hundred unique answers. "Spiritual" is pertaining to or consisting of spirit. The spirit is our soul, our being, separate from our body. "Awakening" is reviving to make conscious or alert; aware. Many call this enlightenment. You could say a spiritual awakening is opening the eyes of your soul.

A spiritual awakening to me is experiencing the Holy Spirit in my life; the fruits of the Spirit. It's seeing God's everyday miracles, His beauty and creation. It's receiving Jesus Christ's freely given gifts of grace, mercy and salvation. It's accepting and embracing His unconditional love, forgiveness, and compassion towards me. It's feeling the peace and calm while in the eye of a life storm. When I hear His voice, it is an awakening. I've had many spiritual awakenings as a result of working these steps – some little and some big – each special and promising.

We've worked and continue to work these steps, and as we do, blockage is removed: those things that separate us from God, the lingering after-effects from experiencing our Nevers. The gap between God and us gets smaller, bridged through Jesus Christ, allowing us to receive more of God, the Spirit. He dwells within us; He brings a fire to ignite the candle in our soul. This is our spiritual awakening, and we become a light as His Spirit works in us and through us. The fruits of the Spirit equip us and give us the strength to "try to carry this message to others."

Are you still willing? For us to effectively implement this tool we must maintain the same attitude of willingness that has allowed us to get to this place. The reason I ask this question is because this step says, "tried" – we "try" to carry this message to others. If I could remove that word, I would. I don't like the word "try." I see this word as being a potential cop-out or an excuse to put it on the back burner. The word "try" is not an intentional word that means action. It's a weak word that communicates, *I might,* or *if I feel like it,* or *if it's easy,* or *if I don't have to do something that exists outside of my comfort zone.* Let's remove the word "try" and decide to carry this message. Let's commit to doing our best. If we are deliberate with this step, we will experience joy in living.

You may be asking the following questions:

How do we carry this message? We carry by sharing and connecting with others. Each of our platforms is unique; yours will be unique to you. Seek God's will for the method. We carry the message through giving, loving, and showing compassion. We carry it by living these steps, by living transparent lives, and by continuing to implement these tools in our daily walk. We are a light that transmits into the lives of others; we shine and light our world. We take action by making a phone call or by writing a letter with words of encouragement to someone. We carry it through conversations, through hugs, and smiles. We look for what needs to be done – we volunteer, we sing in choir, serve, clean, plan – we teach, we write, we speak.

> *"Remember that the happiest people are not those getting more, but those giving more."*
>
> —H. JACKSON BROWN, JR.

What is our message? Our life becomes our message. Our message is our personal experience, our strength, and hope. It's affirming God's goodness. As we overcome our Nevers, refine our lives, and become who God created us to be, our message evolves and grows with us. We seek God through prayer and meditation asking Him to lead us and guide us – we ask Him to make our message known to us. For some of us, we share our victories and our struggles. We share our tools that helped us, we share our faith, we share our stories, God's grace and love. We share what's on our heart and what we feel comfortable and led to share.

Who do we carry our message to? To others; to one or many. We shine our light in our relationships, in our homes, at our workplaces, in checkout lines, and over the phone – with anyone we come in contact with. We look for opportunities as doors open for us to share our message. Again, we seek God's will; we ask Him what His plan is for our lives. Through prayer and meditation we seek His guidance, asking Him to lead us to those needing to hear our message. Our goal is to be of service, to be helpful, to plant seeds. We can shine our light by being the "good Samaritan" or by performing "random acts of kindness." As you shine your light, as your light becomes brighter, as God continues to work out His plan and purpose in your life, others will be drawn to you. There is warmth and comfort when we are close to the flame.

I want to caution you about something. We can be so excited about this phase in our development – our new tools, our spiritual awakening, this new pair of "glasses" we've been given – that we tell others what we think they should do. Think about a child who gets a new toy. She wants to share it with everyone, she's excited, she thinks that everyone needs to have one just like it. She jumps up and down, saying, "Look at me! Look at me! This makes me happy, you will be happy too!"

These steps and this toolbox that you now carry are about attraction, not promotion. Remember, people will be drawn to the light.

Don't tell others what you think they should do. Do not pressure, attempt to control, or manipulate others to believe what you believe. Others have to want help and be willing to help themselves – which means they need to take action, do hard things, and desire change. Our attitude is crucial in our delivery. Have an attitude of enthusiasm, celebration, victory, forgiveness, and healing. Focus on planting these seeds.

Each morning I whisper little prayers like, "Father, Thank You for Your love, guidance, blessings, and strength. May Your light shine through me and direct my path today." Or "Jesus, as I meet and interact with others today, may they see You. Give me the words to say, shine through me." I embrace the concept of living one day at a time for the rest of my life. Each day, each moment I live is a gift. You never know when God could use you to be a blessing in the life of others. You don't want to miss those opportunities by imposing your agenda on them. Focus on attraction, not promotion. When the time is right, the seed you planted will be watered. You may never see this phase of development in the other person, and that's okay – keep planting seeds.

There are three stumbling blocks that can prevent us from shining our light:

1. We stop implementing some or all the tools in our toolbox. This could happen if we rest on our laurels thinking that "we've arrived," life is good, everything is going smoothly, and we can just sit back and relax. If we are not taking action to move forward, if we stop working one or more of these steps and do not continue to grow emotionally and spiritually, our spiritual light can dull and blockage can start to build up between us and God.

2. We don't give credit where credit is due. When selfishness, our pride, and our egos step up, we may begin to think that it is through our own strength that we are growing, that we alone have discovered truth, that we alone can love, and experience joy. When we remove God from the equation, our spiritual flame flickers. He is the fuel that gives our flame its vibrant light. We must never think that we could come this far and continue on without His presence. Our worship is to give God all the glory.

3. We experience hardship or setbacks; we make mistakes, we tire. The reality is that life happens. We will always continue to be human, and we will always make mistakes. There will always be challenging circumstances; loved ones may die, we may experience life-altering circumstances that trip us up. Others around us may never change; in short, life will not be perfect. We will experience growing pains; we will get hurt, wounded, or broken. With each of these examples we must turn to our toolbox full of valuable tools, and decide what will help us pull through. Spirituality means growth through pain, not escape from pain. We will have quiet seasons where we need to rest, to be still, and that's okay – but don't let the obstacles of life derail you. Do your best to take baby steps forward, embracing God's grace and mercy, and seeking Him through prayer and meditation.

To prevent these stumbling blocks from hindering the progress on our journey, our focus needs to remain on ourselves, on our side of the street, in our own backyard. We may like to change all sorts of people, but our willingness to change and grow is only our own; others need to have their own will to change and grow.

We are to "practice these principles in all of our affairs." We learn as we practice. We put our spiritual growth first. We will all fall short of implementing these tools on a consistent basis, but the crucial element is that we remain willing to take action, look in the mirror, and persevere. This is hard work. We are in the process of becoming: like a caterpillar that transforms into a butterfly, we are equipped, we have everything within to become what we are supposed to be. We focus on ourselves. The answers are not somewhere outside of you. They are not about others changing, or circumstances getting better, but from within the framework of our being, our attitudes.

The beautiful gift that I've received and continue to receive is seeing God's will and plan for my life unfolding daily. You see, I never wanted to write a book, so with writing this book I'm actually accomplishing a good Never. I was lying in bed with my husband last week, having a "pillow talk" (I love pillow talks, they are my favorite), and he said, "I'm so proud of you, you're accomplishing one of your dreams."

I got very emotional; my eyes welled up with tears because it never was one of my dreams. Writing a book, honestly, is something I never thought I could do. *I can't do that! I'm not a writer! I would never write a book, are you kidding me? No! That's not even on the bucket list.*

But as I shared my story with people in my life, those I've mentored, coached and spoken to, I described my story as a journey of "Overcoming the Nevers." People could relate to this concept and what I found was that I was not alone. That's a comforting feeling, right? That's when the book idea came into my head. It was just an idea – that's it! Nothing more, or so I thought.

Just like anything in life, including our thoughts, what we feed grows. The seed was planted. I continued to talk about it. Others encouraged me to do it. Before I knew it, the idea grew. I had enough written about this idea to bring it with confidence to someone who could help me. I submitted a brief synopsis of my book, and here I am sitting at Starbucks on the 4th of July, wrapping up the last chapter.

It really was not my plan to write a book. I'm not capable of developing such a plan. But, here I sit with a smile on my face and joy in my heart, thinking about how I'm liking this plan which I truly believe to be His plan: God's Plan for me.

I'm passionate about helping others. I see people as equal. I see people as little souls that are wounded, and that is where I used to be – wounded. I feel that I've got a great toolbox, with one solution that can bring restoration and healing to others. The toolbox doesn't belong to me. It's something that God has shown me and allowed me to experience, through A.A. and other things. This book is a big part of my 12th Step – I'm walking in obedience to what God has laid on my heart. This is one way He has called me to be a light. I can't talk to every single person but, through this book, I feel like the message can be shared. Maybe I'll have an opportunity to talk to people I wouldn't have otherwise have been able to reach. Maybe lives will be impacted because of the book. My life has been impacted through the writing of this book. It has stretched me, refined me, and taught me more about patience, obedience, willingness, and vulnerability; *Oh my goodness, I'm putting this out there.*

Does this mean I'm done? No way. Just like you, I have to keep working the steps.

I just might be a few months ahead of you right now, maybe I've done this a few more times than you, but I'm still going through it and I'm still doing it, living these tools. So, what's next for me is just to continue to grow, and to continue to help others by sharing my story.

I feel like God's made it very clear to me that this is what He wants me to do. He doesn't want me to hide my light underneath a bushel, NO! He wants me to be a light in my community, in my world, whatever my sphere is, whether big or small. I'm responsible for that. My desire is to remain willing, apply these tools into my daily life, to love others.

How far does your responsibility to others go in this step? That's between you and God. Somebody else who's gotten to this point, who has gone through the work of these 12 steps, and wants to be a light to the world or the community, will have a different experience than mine. It doesn't have to be big and bold and doesn't have to be writing a book; it doesn't have to be public speaking. It can be at work; it can be being a light to your children. It could be being a better wife, or husband. Whatever it is, it's becoming who God created us to be.

I don't know who God created you to be. You'll find out if you go through this process, just like I did. If somebody had shown me a film two years ago of me today, sitting here writing a book, I would've boldly declared, "Ummm, you've got the wrong girl." I only have a limited view of what God's plan is for me. I don't know what the future holds. I don't even know where I'm going to be six months from now. All that I know for certain is that I need to shine His light on my next step and take it; to walk in obedience, walk in faith, continue to look at my side of the street, continue to make amends, continue to be humble, to take responsibility and to be aware.

We become reflectors and this is our time and our opportunity to give the glory to God. This is when we give credit where credit is due. We share our nothingness without the Source, and give a testimony of how the Source is available to anyone who surrenders and realizes that they are nothing without their Creator who loves and has a special, unique plan drafted specifically for them. My plan is not your plan, and your plan is not another person's plan. We are all a part of one body created to fulfill a specific purpose in God's overall plan.

"Sing to God, everyone and everything! Get out his salvation news every day! Publish his glory among the godless nations, his wonders to all races and religions. And why? Because God is great—well worth praising! No god or goddess comes close in honor. All the popular gods are stuff of nonsense, but God made the cosmos! Splendor and majesty flow out of him, strength and joy fill his place." 1 Chronicles 16:23-27 (The Message)

I don't want to forget about giving credit where credit's due because I couldn't have done any of this on my own. I made a mess. I am nothing without God and everything with Him.

"Shine on!" And let your light touch others, as I hope mine has touched you.

Keeping it Personal

1. Have you noticed your desires mirroring your actions? Are you pleased with them?

2. What spiritual awakenings have you had as a result of working these 12 steps?

3. What works have resulted from your action-packed faith?

4. Have you eliminated the word "try"? Have you determined to "do"?

5. List ten people that immediately come to your mind with whom you want to share your message, through attraction, not promotion – and to whom you want to be a LIGHT!

The Willingness Toolbox
Tool: Step

1. **ACCEPTANCE :** We admitted we were powerless over {life, others, emotions} alcohol — that our lives had become unmanageable.

2. **FAITH :** Came to believe that a Power greater than ourselves could restore us to sanity.

3. **SURRENDER :** Made a decision to turn our will and our lives over to the care of God as we understood Him.

4. **COURAGE :** Made a searching and fearless moral inventory of ourselves.

5. **ADMISSION :** Admitted to God, to ourselves, and to another human being the exact nature of our wrongs.

6. **TRANSFORMATION :** Were entirely ready to have God remove all these defects of character.

7. **HUMILITY :** Humbly asked Him to remove our shortcomings.

8. **RESPONSIBILITY :** Made a list of all persons we had harmed, and became willing to make amends to them all.

9. **RESTORATION :** Made direct amends to such people wherever possible, except when to do so would injure them or others.

10. **CLARITY :** Continued to take personal inventory and when we were wrong promptly admitted it.

11. **AWARENESS :** Sought through prayer and meditation to improve our conscious contact with God, as we understood Him, praying only for knowledge of His will for us and the power to carry that out.

12. **LIGHT :** Having had a spiritual awakening as the result of these Steps, we tried to carry this message to {others} alcoholics, and to practice these principles in all our affairs.

Don't Let Your Journey Stop Here…

Continue to walk with me to overcome your nevers, refining yourself and becoming the true person you are.

Stay Connected with me by joining our Facebook and Twitter pages at **facebook.com/terijohnson.writes, facebook.com/keepingitpersonal** and **twitter.com/keepitpersonal**

Visit my website at **keepingitpersonal.com**

❋ We invite you to join our daily *KIP* network to begin receiving your daily inspirational message.

❋ To continue your journey we offer *Life Coaching* where together we will peel back the layers and explore your core values, goals, commitments, life roles, and passions.

❋ Be a part of our *Ultimate Journey Program* where in this life transforming process we will focus on connecting knowledge to the heart of who you were created to be. We invite you to watch our video testimonials of what other clients have experienced.

Visit **terijohnson.com** to preview my inspiring speaking topics, *Who Are You Really, No Baggage, Know Bliss* and *Garden and Grow.* Where your audience members will learn the power of releasing and forgiving, embrace the place they are in to feel empowered and to nourish their lives to begin producing a great harvest…

Discover Truth, Embrace Love, Experience Joy
Teri Johnson

CPSIA information can be obtained
at www.ICGtesting.com
Printed in the USA
BVHW05s1432180718
521945BV00023B/863/P

9 781599 322513